PRODIGY PUBLISHED

Zlatan Demirović
Founder,
Editor in Chief

Board of advisors:

Dr. Jernail Singh Anand-editorial advisor-India

Dr. Molly Joseph- editorial advisor-India

Shikdar Mohammed Kibtiah-editorial advisor-Bangladesh

Prof. Dr. Joseph Spence Sr-editorial advisor-USA

Dr. Maria Do Sameiro Barroso-editorial advisor-Portugal

Joan Josep Barcelo-editorial advisor-Spain/Italy

Slava Božičević-editorial advisor-Croatia/Balkan

Mircea Dan Duta-editorial advisor-Romania/East Europe

Lidia Chiarelli-editorial advisor-Italy

Hannie Rouweler-editorial advisor-Netherlands

Shoshana Vegh- editorial advisor-Israel

Prodigy Magazine - March 2025

CONTENTS

BOOK REVIEWS

ESSAYS

POEMS

INTERVIEWS

SELF-HEALING

Prodigy Magazine - March 2025

ZLATAN DEMIROVIĆ: EDITORIAL DESK & PREFACE

BOOK REVIEW

SHIKDAR MOHAMMED KIBRIAH, Bangladesh

(Aestheticism and Philosophy of Art, Part: 9…)

ESSAYS

TAGHRID BOU MERHI, HOPE: THE LIGHT THAT GUIDES US

ZLATINA SADRAZANOVA, HOPE

ELIZA BACH, HOPE IS IMMORTAL

S AFROSE, HOPE, THIS TIME

MAJA MILOJKOVIĆ, **HOPE: A BEACON IN TIMES OF UNCERTAINTY**

SERPİL KAYA, HOPE, A SHARP CRY

SLAVA BOŽIČEVIĆ, MY HOPE AND DREAM OF THE FUTURE WORLD

ALEKHA PRASAD MOHARANA, HOPE

FARZANEH DORRI, HOPE

POEMS

ZLATAN DEMIROVIĆ, USA
SHIRLEY SMOTHERS, USA
JAMES COBURN, USA
BILL STOKES, USA/Alaska
JOAN JOSEP BARCELO, Italy / Spain
LIDIA CHIARELLI, Italy
ADA RIZZO, Italy
IVAN POZZONI, Italy
SERENA ROSSI, Italy
MARIA ERRICO, Italy
SABRINA MORELLI, Italy
ANGELA KOSTA, Albania/Italy
ELISA MASCIA, Italy
CONCETTA LA PLACA, Italy
Dr. JERNAIL S AANAND, India
Dr. MOLLY JOSEPH, India
BHAGIRATH CHOUDHARI, India
Amb. PRIYANKA NEOGI, India
SANKHA RANJAN PATRA, India
ASHOK CHAKRAVARTHY THOLANA, India
Dr. KANWALPREET BAIDWAN, India
GARGI SIDANA, India
Dr. PERWAIZ SHAHARYAR, India
Dr. RAKESH CHANDRA, India
RAJASHREE MOHAPATRA, India
ASOK DAS, India
Dr. ZAINUL HUSAIN, India
ANJALI DENANDEE, MOM, India
BALACHANDRAN NAIR, India
ABEERA MIRZA, India
MD EJAJ AHAMED, India
PRIYATOSH DAS, India
Prof. Dr. LAXMIKANTA DASH, India
SUDIPTA MISHRA, India

SHIKDAR MOHAMMED KIBRIAH, Bangladesh
RANA ZAMAN, Bangladesh
S AFROSE, Bangladesh
SAYEEDA AZIZ CHOWDHURY, Bangladesh
NILOY RAFIQ, Bangladesh
TAPAS DEY, Bangladesh
AKLIMA ANKHI, Bangladesh
ALAM MAHBUB, Bangladesh
SANTOSH KUMAR POKHAREL, Nepal
TIL KUMARI SHARMA, Nepal
RENUKA BHATTA, Nepal
ANGELA CHRONOPOULOU, Greece
EFTICHIA KAPARDELI, Greece
CHRISTOS DIKBASANIS, Greece
PETROS KYRIAKOU VELOUDAS, Greece
XRYSOULA FOUFA, Greece
ROZALIA ALEKSANDROVA, Bulgaria
ZLATINA SADRAZANOVA, Bulgaria
NATALIJA NEDYALKOVA, Bulgaria
NADYA RAYKOVA, Bulgaria
YORDANKA GETSOVA, Bulgaria
TSVETA MIHAYLOVA, Bulgaria
KIEU BICH HAU, Vietnam
VAN DIEN, Vietnam
LE DUYEN, Vietnam
HONG NGOC CHAU, Vietnam
Dr. ANA STJELJA, (ANA S. GAD), Serbia
TANJA AJTIĆ, Serbia/Canada
IRENA JOVANOVIĆ, Serbia
ZDENKO ĆURKOVIĆ, Croatia
MARINA ŠUR PUHLOVSKI, Croatia
DANIJELA ĆUK, Croatia
FROSINA TASEVSKA, Macedonia
ELIZABETA DONČEVSKA- LUŠIN, Macedonia
ČEDOMIR B. ŠOPKIĆ, Macedonia
IBRAHIM HONJO, Bosnia and Herzegovina/Canada

ENSAR BUKARIĆ, Bosnia and Herzegovina
CVIJA PERANOVIĆ KOJIĆ, Bosnia and Herzegovina/Austria
ALEKSANDRA VUJISIĆ, Montenegro
EWITH BAHAR, Indonesia
WIRJA TAUFAN, Indonesia
ERNESTO P. SANTIAGO, Philippines
MARLON SALEM GRUEZO-BONDROFF, Philippines/USA
RUT VARGAS-VIVAS, Colombia/USA
LASKIAF AMORTEGUI, Colombia
KUMARKHANOVA AINUR SERIKOVNA, Kazakhstan
DINA ORAZ, Kazakhstan
ELHAM HAMEDI, Iran/Italy
FARZANEH DORRI, Iran/Denmark
SHOSHANA VEGH, Israel
HANITA ROZEN, Israel
ISAAC COHEN, Israel
Dr. MARIA DO SAMEIRO BARROSO, Portugal
DR.HC. NATALIE BISSO, Germany
LEO ACOSTA, Nicaragua
CORINA JUNGHIATU, Romania
TETIANA HRYTSAN-CHONKA, Ukraine
FOLAJIMI NOTCH SHOAGA, Nigeria
NORMA MARINA SOLIS ZAVALA, Peru
SANDRINE DAVIN, France
Ph.Dr. MA YONGBO, China
ANNA MARIA MICKIEWICZ, England
OLA GLUSTIKOVA, Slovakia
YOUCEF MEBARKIA, Algeria
HUSSEIN HABASCH, Kurdistan
GABRIEL S. WEAH, Liberia
DEBRA JOE, United Arab Emirates
NIKOLLË LOKA, Albania
SAJID HUSSAIN, Pakistan
ELMAYA CABBAROVA, Azerbaijan

INTERVIEW

ROZALIA ALEKSANDROVA, Bulgaria

with

DINCHO CHOBANOV, Bulgaria

SELF-HEALING

Dr. ANA STJELJA, (ANA S. GAD), Serbia: AEZE MOHAMMED HASSAN: Art as a Path to Healing

FOLAJIMI NOTCH SHOAGA, Nigeria: SELF-HEALING ON HOPE

FROSINA TASEVSKA, Macedonia: PERSISTENCE IN THE FIELD OF THOUGHT

S AFROSE, Bangladesh: BE POSITIVE

FARZANEH DORRI, Iran/Denmark: THOUGHTS AND FEELINGS

EDITORIAL DESK

Greetings, dear friends, brothers, sisters, poetry-literature, and hilosophy lovers!

Welcome to the twelfth, Prodigy Magazine edition, March 2025.

This is another milestone in our mission of uplifting human essence, in reaching the final goal of ultimate raising of global consciousness. We are here to save our real human source and push ahead against distraction. For that, we use the most powerful weapons, as a gift from the Universe: the power of creation, talent, inspiration, intuition, passion for truth linked with universal knowledge, real education, and the mindset of winners!

Our ideology is affirmation of joy, love for humanity as a part of Mother Nature, truth of real existence aligned with Universal laws!

Be a critic of this performance, just as a real critic of yourself, acting as a child willing to express a pure creative inner world!

We made it together, challenging our abilities for the most valuable achievements!

Sincerely yours,

Zlatan Demirović
Founder

Prodigy Magazine - March 2025

PREFACE:

Dear reader, this is our new, March 2025 edition of our bimensal magazin, which started in June 2022.

The main goal of our continuous improvement is to make periodic changes, increase the efficiency, accuracy, and finaly, to be creative.

This way we set up a stage for more extensive quality promotion.

As it's not possible to put "all in one box", it opens a possibility for long-term creative process.

We do it consistently, with no pressure, and no concern of missing something. There is room enough for creative adventures in infinite Mandala Circle.

Truth is under attack, and our mission should be, not only to give up of fake history books, but to remove the dust from ancient divine guidelines for enlightenment.

In this issue we are demonstrating our commitment and ability to work together, creating just one poem, as a unison voice as a collective message of hundred plus authors from all around the World.

Aware of what we are facing in a very short future, we must unite in one general idea of breaking all the paradigms that we are carrying as a collar around our necks.

Individually, we are not strong enough, but collectively we can make a change. This switch is already happening but it's going very slow, so we are here to push it as much as possible.

How can we do it?

We can't go to institutions, trying to make the changes, and can't convince any leader, not to do what he's well paid for!

As we all know, sick body is occasionally treated from material plane, but very often unsuccessfully.

Spiritual plane is where disease came, and the cure should go there.

We are spiritual beings and should address our message to the same field.

Higher consciousness is one which resonates, reversing to us.

Just, do what you already started!

Great thinker, Napoleon Hill, used to call it mastermind alliance, which is condicio sine qua non, for any success.

Hope you'll love our new columna, SELF-HEALING. Enjoy in reading lyrics and inspirational insights of big literary names, and glimmer of hope in CIVILIZATION TESLYANA!

Zlatan Demirović

GREAT NEWS FOR PAINTERS!

All painters already published in Prodigy Magazine, are automatically prequalified for a membership in the new PRODIGY ONLINE AUCTION GALERY!

For more info, just send your email with a subject: POAG MEMBER

on:

prodigypublished@gmail.com

and you'll receive introductory info.

Zlatan Demirović

Collage: SAVING THE EARTH, Ljiljana Stjelja, Serbia

BOOK REVIEW

SHIKDAR MOHAMMED KIBRIAH, Bangladesh

AESTHETICISM AND PHILOSOPHY OF ART, Part: 9

My Aesthetic -1:

Hegel said, Art is the sensuous presentation of the Absolute. Again, according to the neo-idealist Benedetto Croce, if "Expression is art" and "Any subject is the subject of artwork", then it can be said that the metaphysical truth of each subject is part of the ultimate truth and artistic expression is the expression of the Absolute. And the artist is the representative of the Supreme. Therefore, the expression of perfection is the artistic desire of the true artist. Metaphysical knowledge is impossible without the concept of the Absolute. Because the sequence of causality cannot continue indefinitely. Absolute is the cause of the cause — the final cause. Without this being, the world is false, disordered, and ugly. There is no space of evil in the absolute. The master of evil is the liberated human being. Since the Absolute is truth and auspicious and true beauty is the manifestation of the Absolute, therefore, true beauty is auspicious truth. Art reflects it.

The overall creative, independent, and virtuous existence of man is determined by the three great values of truth, goodness, and beauty. There is no denying this truth-feeling in reality. These are inevitably pragmatic considerations of human philosophy. Whatever the nature of their independent and individual existence in the pure sense, pragmatically they are closely related. For example, the Absolute is truth, but if that being is neither the source of beauty nor the benevolent effect, then this meaningless being has no "human need." And if it is not related to human needs in any way, why will the human soul be inspired by such philosophy or art-literature practice? If nothing else, at least the need for self-satisfaction must exist. And true self-satisfaction or happiness does not come selfishly or ignoring others.

At least that much happiness can be called self-happiness, which, whether it causes the happiness of others or not, at least does not cause unhappiness. If self-happiness is associated with the all-happiness and turns into universal happiness, then it is undoubtedly great happiness. Thus, an art pleasure or aesthetic satisfaction that causes mere self-satisfaction without causing others' dissatisfaction is definitely art. But if it causes satisfaction for others as well as self-satisfaction, then it is great art. So the artist is not exempt. (continued)

©® **Shikdar Mohammed Kibriah**

To be continued...

Collage: **A SPARK IN THE EYE OF THE IDEAS**, Ljiljana Stjelja, Serbia

HOPE

ESSAYS

TAGHRID BOU MERHI, Lebanon/Brazil

HOPE: THE LIGHT THAT GUIDES US

Hope is one of the most profound and essential human emotions. It is the invisible force that pushes people forward in times of adversity, the beacon of light that shines through the darkest nights. Hope is not merely wishful thinking; it is an inner conviction that things will improve, that difficulties can be overcome, and that tomorrow holds new possibilities. It fuels resilience, inspires courage, and gives meaning to human existence. Without hope, individuals and societies would be lost in despair, unable to move beyond their present challenges.

Throughout history, hope has been the driving force behind some of the most remarkable human achievements. It has given strength to those suffering under oppression, has lifted the spirits of those battling illness, and has encouraged explorers, inventors, and revolutionaries to strive for a better world. Hope is what kept prisoners of war believing in freedom, what helped civil rights leaders fight for justice, and what allows people facing personal hardships to persevere.

Consider the stories of those who have triumphed over adversity. Nelson Mandela, for instance, endured 27 years of imprisonment in South Africa's Robben Island. Despite the isolation, he never lost hope in the dream of a free and equal nation. His hope was not just passive optimism but an active force that kept him determined and prepared for the moment when change would become possible. Upon his release, his hope materialized into action, leading to the dismantling of apartheid and the establishment of a democratic South Africa.

Similarly, hope sustains people during personal struggles. A cancer patient undergoing chemotherapy, a student struggling with academic pressures, or a refugee seeking safety—all rely on hope to endure their difficulties. It is the belief that tomorrow might bring relief, progress, or new opportunities that prevents despair from taking hold.

Hope is more than just a survival mechanism; it is also a catalyst for change and innovation. Many great discoveries and advancements in science, technology, and medicine have been fueled by hope. Scientists hoping for medical breakthroughs work tirelessly to find cures for diseases. Inventors driven by the hope of improving lives create new technologies. Leaders inspired by hope bring about social transformations. Martin Luther King Jr., in his famous "I Have a Dream" speech, spoke of a hopeful vision where people would not be judged by the color of their skin but by their character. His hope was not blind optimism but a deep-seated belief in justice, equality, and human dignity. This hope led to the Civil Rights Movement, which brought about legislative and social changes in the United States.

Hope also plays a vital role in shaping the future. Young people entering the workforce, parents raising children, and communities rebuilding after disasters all rely on hope. It gives people the confidence to invest in education, careers, and relationships, believing that their efforts will lead to a better tomorrow. Hope is what encourages societies to tackle challenges such as climate change, poverty, and inequality, envisioning a future where progress is possible.

While hope is powerful, it is also fragile. Life's hardships, repeated failures, or prolonged suffering can weaken hope, leading to despair. In such moments, external support, faith, and resilience play crucial roles in reigniting hope. Literature, music, religion, and personal relationships often serve as sources of renewed hope for those struggling.

At the same time, hope is remarkably resilient. It can be rekindled by a small act of kindness, an inspiring story, or even a simple sunrise that signals a new day. People who lose everything in natural disasters still find hope in the support of strangers. Those who face devastating losses discover hope in new beginnings. The ability of hope to survive even in the bleakest circumstances is a testament to its deep-rooted significance in human life.

Hope is more than just an emotion; it is a way of life. It teaches us to look beyond the present moment, to believe in possibilities, and to work towards a brighter future. Whether facing personal struggles, societal challenges, or global crises, hope remains the foundation of human perseverance and progress.

To cultivate hope, one must nurture optimism, seek inspiration, and take positive action. Acts of kindness, expressions of gratitude, and faith in humanity all contribute to sustaining hope. As long as people hold on to hope, no challenge is insurmountable, and no dream is unattainable. It is hope that keeps the world moving forward, reminding us that no matter how dark the night, the dawn is always within reach.

©® **Taghrid Bou Merhi**

ZLATINA SADRAZANOVA, Bulgaria

HOPE

They say that each person is a small Universe. And that is true. There are no two individuals with the same consciousness. Therefore, each person is extremely valuable. Every time when I think about who I am, what I was, what I will be, different emotions, moments, and people come to my mind…

Everything I want to do is always monitored, approved or criticized by other people. But in fact, I am a human being, I have hopes, and nothing human is alien to me!

People are afraid of the ones who know themselves. They radiate some kind of power, have an aura of magnetism, charisma that takes young people out of the prison of tradition. One, two, one two … money and power put us in the meat grinder … Malice, hatred, cruelty, pain!

In all of its varieties and locations.

You yourself must choose the path you will take. This makes you free. Without freedom, a person would become an impersonal being.

I come alone and I will go alone. I come to get to know love not from formulas, but at the risk of getting burn wounds. Even if they are incurable. To overcome myself, to break the way of thinking and behaving I have been taught for centuries. To break my instinctive girlish fear and stupid shame. To trample on prejudices, doubts, stiffness. This is equal to a revolution.

I look at the world from above with liberated eyes… Life and time are like a river, you can never touch the same drop twice, because the drop that passes by you will never come again.

Enjoy every moment of life, it will never be repeated. Happiness, another important existential problem, is perhaps the goal that everyone strives for. Because, if you find true happiness, then you have also found the meaning of your existence. And happiness can be found in conscious freedom and love. That one, the unearthly love that makes you feel alive. That one you believe in and hope it will come to you one day.

I am not bored. I enter a bar. Through the window I can see a happy couple. They are talking to each other. Holding their hands, intoxicated by the moment. I am happy for them … there are happy people. I will paint something like that, impressionistic … with rain and passion. When the drop running down the nose of the one of them and the happy tears of the other whisper gently and make plans for the future …

A happy person is the one who has learned to admire, not to envy, to follow, but not to imitate. To praise, but not to flatter, to lead, but not to manipulate …

To live for a hope for a better life.

©® **Zlatina Sadrazanova**

ELIZA BACH, Denmark

HOPE IS IMMORTAL

In the myth of hope, it is said that Prometheus stole fire from the gods. The gods took revenge, turning the goddess Pandora into an earthling. They sent a gift to people with her. Prometheus fell in love with her and the box sent as a gift by the gods. He married her. He eagerly opened Pandora's box. From the box, in the form of animals, all the evils came out and filled the earth. The perfection that was on Earth was unbalanced. When Prometheus saw all the evil coming out of the box, he quickly closed it. But it was too late. Diseases, envy, wars and the rest of the evil took their place in people.

The only being that remained in the box sent by the gods was a bird. One of its wings was broken, about to fly into nothingness.

When the darkness of suffering fills the life of man, only one guiding star remains and appears to the human soul to save it. The light of the star is called Hope.

The gods were revengeful, but they were also merciful. If people want to be like the gods, they must become strong and wise at the same time. They must reach the level of consciousness that is obtained through merit, by knowing how and when to use fire.

Hope is the oxygen of existence. Life feeds on hope from one moment to the next, from one hour to the next, from one year to the next, from light years to thousands of light years. By inspiring hope, you keep faith alive. Faith heals the broken wing of hope. It makes you strong and restores your trust in love. Love brings the wisdom of balance into the human being and from there, between people. Hope never stands alone. From the non-being of the sky of the human heart flies into the being of faith in goodness and gives birth to love. Love gives meaning to life. Its fire burns to create.

Hope comes from the immortal hand and holds in a mortal human heart, a longing to fly to an immortal portal.

©® **Eliza Bach**

S AFROSE, Bangladesh

HOPE, THIS TIME

Can you see the light?
No.
Why dear?
What's wrong?
Believe, you can make if you determined.
Hope this time, a sky with so many stars. Within all, you will be the one.
Just accept and love and cherish this in the deepest heart.
Phone is ringing.
Hello!it's Tesla.
Who are you?
Hello Tesla! I'm your dream. I am your winning smile. How are you?
Can you meet with me?
Tesla: I don't understand what are you saying?
My winning smile?
How can you say this?
Listen, You aren't a loser dear. I know you from the very past. You love all. You do your best. But sometimes a negative feedback. You lose your strength. And then... You act as a loser.
Why and why?

Tesla, think about that hard times. You couldn't talk, walk, eat and so...
You tried and tried and then, you got the desired result.
That's your winning smile.

You can follow that again. Nourish hope in the deepest mind. You must be the winner At Last.
Tesla: Oh no!
Thanks for recalling those things.
Definitely I will conquer my state.
Yes! I can. I have to do. I must be...

©® S Afrose

MAJA MILOJKOVIĆ, Serbia

HOPE: A BEACON IN TIMES OF UNCERTAINTY

In moments when challenges seem insurmountable and the world is shrouded in uncertainty, hope remains an unquenchable flame illuminating the path to a better future. Although it is but a single word, its significance is vast, permeating all aspects of human existence.
Hope propels us to rise after falls, to believe in a brighter tomorrow, and to strive for our dreams despite obstacles. It is the inner strength that helps us overcome fears and face the unknown. Without hope, life would be devoid of color, and our endeavors would lose meaning.
In difficult times, when problems appear insurmountable, hope becomes a crucial support. It reminds us that, while we cannot control everything happening around us, we can control our attitude and approach. Through hope, we find the courage to confront challenges and persist in our efforts.
Philosopher Jürgen Moltmann, in his work "Theology of Hope," emphasizes that hope is not merely the anticipation of a better tomorrow but an active force that motivates us to act in the present to shape the future.
In conclusion, hope is an inseparable part of the human experience. It guides us through the darkest moments and inspires us to strive for a brighter future. In a world full of uncertainty, hope remains our faithful companion, reminding us that, regardless of circumstances, there is always the possibility for positive change.

©® **Maja Milojković**

SERPİL KAYA, Turkey

HOPE, A SHARP CRY

After walking barefoot for miles through thorny paths, rocky and treacherous roads, and after being covered in blood up to your knees, it meant waiting for the golden yellow glimmers of the newly rising day from the crimson and purple horizon of the setting sun; Hope. Even when you were knee-deep in the mire, with your hands and face covered in mud, the sun inside you would still warm you gently. It was to imagine that in a gentle breeze, the scent of the man you loved would come and make your nose tingle, yet despite that, you would savor that bittersweet pain to the very last drop. It was being able to dance the dance of love in a fire-red dress, getting drunk in his arms. It meant being able to write the story of being reborn in love again and again from the ruins of an emotional earthquake with a love-red pen. And hope: Despite all the dark waters and thorny paths, it was the sharpest cry of being able to stand tall even if we remained bloodied and bruised.

Most importantly, hope was the name of holding on to life and the days to come without any reason. It meant knowing that every dark night would have a morning and the sun would rise again. Since pink flowers could bloom from brown branches, there was always hope in life.

Because the end of every winter was spring. At the end of every frost is a warm yellow sun.

©® **Serpil Kaya**

SLAVA BOŽIČEVIĆ, Croatia

MY HOPE AND DREAM OF THE FUTURE WORLD

Today's humanity is creating a new era of 21st century life on planet Earth. The reason is the rapid development of new technology and digitalization. The world is at a crossroads, it is changing much more dinamicaly than it was 30-50 years ago. Old systems of life and social behavior are collapsing. For the first time in the history of humanity, a war is being waged against the population of this planet, and the organizers and leaders are mega-rich billionaires who have created a new movement, transhumanism - and this movement operates through digitalization, technology, propaganda, spreading disinformation by corrupt media. This is how fear, threats and insecurity are sown. Fear is the strongest emotion that affects humans.
The world is falling into a trap and is gradually and radically changing towards the *Great Reset*. Humanity must wake up and become aware.
The world has not been created as a game, without meaning and
purpose. Its essential purpose is development, evolution and ascension.
The ultimate goal should be spirituality. "A healthy spiritual life in the world will only begin when the physical, mental, ethical and social life matures, that the diversity of the world is the cultural wealth and that the original truth unites the world"- Sam Harris.
A modern, rational man must be aware of his being, his consciousness and his duty as a citizen of the universe. Difficult tasks await future generations. We have not left them a good world as a legacy. I am ashamed of that. There are good people and

young mature people.
Young people should be better than we've been.
Because they are opposed by a manipulative system, which directs them according to its principles.
The system is built through people, which means that it should be encountered there among them....SO YOU WILL BE GOOD. Every person knows what it is, because their inner moral compass is so tuned. Kindness is the most beautiful color of the soul.
My hope in young people is great. Young forces will, with their spirit and knowledge, defeat this psychopathic elite, which now rules.
Victory is guaranteed to those who have pledged loyalty, truth.
I believe in young people, because they are already proving themselves, they are going to work cheerfully, and with the will to succeed. Young people will have to create new codes of ethics, because ours are outdated and rotten.
We know that the spiritual rise of civilization is unthinkable without ethics and ethical ideals.
My dream for the future world is that humanity, at the peak of evolution, lives in peace and prosperity, without weapons and wars. That love, empathy, kindness is a priority, that art flourishes.
That a quality life reigns on Earth. Because we are all children of God.

©® **Slava Božičević**

ALEKHA PRASAD MOHARANA, India

HOPE

Hope is vital in life Challenges are inevitable in every human life. Hope provides a boost of motivation and faith to face strife. Positive changes come through trust for easy solution. Energy level becomes more to overcome interruption. But soaring hopes sometimes become ineffective. Unsuccess knocks at the door making everything deceptive. Still hope is vital in life to strengthen the brain Desperation will never rise in mind to shatter expectation Hope is a mirage for the pessimistic creature Their ambitions never become fulfilled bringing rapture. Perplexed mind never sees the ray of Prosperity Rather gets disburted without maintaining any sanctity. Proper planning is absolutely necessary to make any hope fructuous Grace of God is an additional boost to make life hilarious. Rely on God with perseverance to effect hope elevated Life will be ambrosial to invirogate divinity.

©® Alekha Prasad Moharana

FARZANEH DORRI, Iran/Denmark

HOPE

Hope is a driving force within us that can give us strength and create change in our lives - and both small and large hopes can give us new perspectives. Hope can grow out of faith or be given to us by another person or the larger community.
Hope exists where there are people who hope. However, in the philosophical and theological traditions, there is far from agreement on how hope should be described: Is hope a virtue that underlies human action, or is it a divine gift? Is hope illusory or life-sustaining?
Hope does not play the same role in all cultural circles, and the very definition of what hope is can be difficult to determine. In everyday speech, hope denotes the confident expectation of something joyful that will occur in the future - without objective certainty. The words hope and expectation are often used interchangeably. But upon closer inspection, there are considerable differences, even though in both cases the person directs his attention to the future.
The fundamental difference is that while expectation involves a rationally justified assumption, hope expresses an existential future orientation. Expectation belongs in the rational sphere of assumptions, which is based on forecasts. The person who hopes, on the other hand, is in relation to surprise.
Religiously, for example, one can hope for miracles, but one cannot expect them. In the world of hope, things are not (always) built on a rational basis.
Finally, hope cannot be neutral and value-free, as expectation can be. Climate scientists expect a global temperature increase, although they hardly hope for it. The person who hopes, on the other hand, always looks forward to the happy outcome.

Even envious hope ("I hope he is not doing well!") rests on the assumption that the bad outcome is happy - for oneself.

Hope provides a surplus in relation to the present. The person who hopes has time to wait, although objective time may be quite short. Hope possesses an inner slowness that can be transformed into quickness as soon as the opportunity for action presents itself. Those who live their lives at high speed get used to relating only to the immediate future, which can be foreseen.

It is difficult to define and measure hope. The fundamental meaning of hope is discovered through its absence, hopelessness. Hope is a quality of human strength that takes the form of a lasting tendency to believe that one's primary desires can be fulfilled despite impulses towards anarchy and anger at dependence. In hope we find an inner flexibility that is capable of both changing oneself and changing the facts along the way.

In this regard, it is a serious deficiency in modern society that it lacks institutions that, like religions, can confirm hope. However, much hope is tied to the subject, the existence of a culture of hope depends on social institutions that can support hope and give it a unifying form and direction.

It is here that the social and religious dimensions of hope can emerge with renewed strength. Hope is a hope for each individual, for their future and for their eternal significance. But hope can also express itself as a hope for others than oneself, a hope that concerns peace and a form of community in which there is room for distinctiveness and peculiarities. Finally, hope can be extended to a hope on behalf of the life of the planet, without which hope could not encompass future generations of people. Thus understood, hope permeates the three spheres of human life: the individual, the community and nature.

©® Farzaneh Dorri

Author of collage: Ljiljana Stjelja, Serbia

HOPE POEMS

HOPE

ZLATAN DEMIROVIĆ, USA

Welcome to the Wonderland!
Enjoy your favorite dream,
compressed into one pill.
Tablet full of hope…
This is your shot!
Dream can start,
and roll over,
only one direction!
This movie is named,
The Seal of The Beast.
Well known journey,
downward-trip, one way ticket.
No hope for individuality,
neither chance for escape.
Vibrational joy on higher level,
blended with defender's miserable
failure.
If you dream some better future,
good luck!
Welcome to the Wonder-world!
Keep your hope for re-creation!

©® **Zlatan Demirović**

HOPE

SHIRLEY SMOTHERS, USA

Even though the Soldier gave his life
to save others his wife will continue.
She will raise their Son
to be a strong man
because she is a strong Woman.
There is always hope.

©® **Shirley Smothers**

Artist: Shirley Smothers
Title: The Price of Freedom
Technique: Watercolor
Size 20X30

HOPE   **JAMES COBURN, USA**

I open the door
to where I was born.
On the table,
poems
beckoning winter, spring,
summer and fall;
changes and I've
endured them all.
Bad candles are put out.
I can still smell their smoke.
I miss loved ones
who taught me to sing.
Fear shall not hold me.
There is love.
Let it speak for me.

©® **James Coburn**

HOPE

BILL STOKES, USA/Alaska

Hurried words written in a feverish pitch so not a single thought is lost and left behind.
As stanzas seem to writhe and coil from the emotions embedded in the words for you to find.
And then you hope.
Several sleepless nights in a row as the raw emotions whirl and churn into words that in turn must find their exact sequence and place.
And when the last thought has been transmuted into line upon line they are as swirls in a cascading waterfall that only go by once and then return to raw emotions shedding their mantle of language as excess baggage space. And now you hope.
Words are but the vehicle that emotions use to hitchhike from my soul to yours
And with an understanding that if you choose, they can pick the lock and set free a flood of emotions behind once frozen doors. And now you hope.
Vivid images are painted one word at a time.
Until the portrait made of emotions is complete and sublime. And now you hope.
And like a painting where the colors are created by layers of tint and hue.
Poems also have layers that must be closely examined before the true meaning of each stanza comes through.
And now you hope.
The journey that the poet invites you to take can create intense pondering, that at night keeps you awake. And now you hope.
Each language is as an isolated island far out to sea for the embedded hidden meanings are nuances trapped by the mother tongue of the poet be. And now you hope.
Hurried words written in a feverish pitch so not a single thought is lost and left behind.
As stanzas seem to writhe and coil from the emotions embedded in the words for you to find.
hope. And now you hope.

©® Bill Stokes

HOPE

JOAN JOSEP BARCELO, Italy / Spain

like that vertigo on the horizon that lives in words
that vertigo halfway between wounds and scars
of sacrifice and pain in labyrinths of silence
right there on the edge of a future that narrows
in a world where life hurts
like those lips bitten by successive autumns
holding my breath with a nameless ardour
I wish to open a window to a moment of hope
hoping that calm will bring warm days back to the soul
in a world where life flourishes
like that vertigo and those lips in the backlit twilight
I will dream of the hope that will dispel fear
and I will wait for time to heal the wounds

©® **Joan Josep Barcelo**

HOPE

LIDIA CHIARELLI, Italy

(from dark to light)

"Hope is the thing with feathers that perches in the soul, and sings the tunes without the words, and never stops at all."

Emily Dickinson

In this time of fog and thick smoke
we walk in intricate labyrinths -
a swirling void surrounds us.
And suddenly a small light makes its way.
First- flickering then - warmer as moved by nuanced sounds.
It is the Hope that returns and finds its path.
Gentle as a feather
moved by the early morning breeze.
A sweet wordless melody that points the way
outlines new days.
And the dawn has a crystal glow.

©® **Lidia Chiarelli**

HOPE

ADA RIZZO, Italy

You are a seed laid upon the heart,
grown sheltered from the rain of life,
a prelude to the future, a beacon for tomorrow.
Not a last resort but a sweet invitation to pause,
a safe harbor from the waves of storms,
a path to explore, step by step.
You are a bold and light flight,
a rhythmic song that pushes forward,
a bridge over a calm sea;
you are a star that guides the nights,
you are a prophetic horizon.

©® **Ada Rizzo**

HOPE **IVAN POZZONI, Italy**

«Fill a bottle with gasoline»
[I feed on life].
«Wrap a rag around the neck of the bottle»
[I think of a solution]
«Wet the rag with gasoline»
[I call out: no answer]
«Ignite the trigger»
[The indignant soul flares up]
«Smash the bottle between your hands»
[The death of craftsmanship]
The instructions, we now live without maps, are stamped in blood
on athenian ostraka, or on cheap Etruscan vases,
on the walls of Pompeii's brothels, or on the plasters of the cells of byzantine hesychasts,
on the bill of exchange of venetian merchants, oron the trenches of the Great War,
passing down / passing down to us from era to era, from millennium to millennium,
from aedican troubadour to cybernetic storytellers,
and they continue to burn the
(in)human, combustible and comburent at the same time,
consuming him in the flames of the inexhaustible fire of art,
that blazes, extinguishing you, without ever burn out.

©® Ivan Pozzoni

HOPE

SERENA ROSSI, Italy

Hope is the scent of narcissus flower in winter that enters my nose
to the city park where dormant nature does not give fruits
until the Spring.
Dark and cold all rotting, it seems a vessel adrift.
And to be near in the solitude of time.

©® **Serena Rossi**

HOPE

MARIA ERRICO, Italy

And they came for me,
the days of adverse Fate,
the days of telluric pain.
The days of the sword that
pierces the Soul...
And the mind that could not
withstand the breathlessness and
seemed to succumb ...
But, from the depths of the Cosmos,
one night a Star exploded, as if
out of nowhere.
Silent maternal Visitor
contemplated me
with Silver Light
that pervaded my afflicted Heart
of unspeakable
HOPE!

©® **Maria Errico**
Translated by Zlatan Demirović

LOVE EXISTES   **SABRINA MORELLI, Italy**

Love exists,
love is true,
a vibrate within
that mystery called soul.
You don't feel it
when it comes in,
you just sense a feeling
that destabilizes every rule.
It confuses you,
it surprises you,
it unites in vertigo skin
and mind inside
a heart that gasps.
You can call him
by his name,
you can shout it
out among millions
of expressions
that don't change
it's destination .
It is unconsciousness,
it is illusion,
it is that indomitable passion
that merges between
the sighs of a magic dance.
Two words to give
that ancient emotion,
love exists,
is not a deception
of reason,
but a flight on layers
of clouds between two halves
of the same drive.

©® **Sabrina Morelli**

HOPE   **ANGELA KOSTA, Albania/Italy**

Hope is the subtle light that darkness challenges
is the here in the heart, even when the world is silent,
is the whisper that in tears, promises
Sprouting rose petals in silence
it is the breeze that the face gently caresses.
Hope is the smile of the eyes
that the fears of challenge,
it is the Supernova that guides us towards the universe
It is the outstretched hand when the path is unsafe
it is salvation, in the stormy ocean of life.
Hope is our solemn courage
Even if the abyss drags us
It's that ray of sunshine, going through the cracks
and inside our soul resides.

©® **Angela Kosta**

THE ROAD IS NOT FINISHED   ELISA MASCIA, Italy

The colors of the sun at dawn are reflected on
the icy road on the walls of purplish red house
with a beating heart and illuminated inside.
It is enough even little of the here and now fresh
air always breathed among green trees high in
the sky you taste every person of nature is in
love.
The colors of purity blend with the green of
hope, the bright red of the burning fire
that from the outside gives chimney beauty
seems to repeat that in all constancy it takes and
enough will never be little.

©® **Elisa Mascia**

LIFE IS HOPE   CONCETTA LA PLACA, Italy

Life has delicate, luminous wings.
It is a fragile thread
that can break
at any time.
It is a dandelion that the breeze
of the harsh seasons
can scatter across the cosmos.
Along its path one must choose
the antidote of love
that neutralises hatred.
Crumbs of love and faith
to moisten
all withered humanity.
Life is always hope and must be painted
in the brightest colours
of our soul.

©® **Concetta La Placa**

THE ISOLATED SUFFERER

Dr. JERNAIL S AANAND, India

Men who lived in joint families
And believed in collective living
Who shared each other's
Joys and sorrows
When there was a celebration
Or when tragedies struck
Were never alone.
It was not easy to tackle man
When he was in the company of his kinsmen.
The forces that wanted him shot down
Studied human behavioural patterns
And soon realized
Man cannot be hunted
So long as he remains in the herd.
A devious plan was hatched
To singularise him.
And the glamorous name of this
Game was individualism.
It was meant to isolate man
Make him lonely
Break customs which united them
Reduce interdependence
Even among couples
Make man stand alone.
Take away the tree from the forest
So that you can strip it at will
And there will not be anyone
To cry over its destiny.
When man is lonely
Nobody around him to sympathize
It is easier to kill his inner being
And reduce him to a body
When faced with questions of survival.
It was essential to cause a chasm
Between man and woman
And then between man and man
Now when each man stands singularised,
He can be handled with deceit.

©® **Jernail S Aanand**

HOPE

Dr. MOLLY JOSEPH, India

Somewhere, cutting across the shards of despair and gloom
the sky clears up slow, hope augurs...
Somewhere, braving the bombing,
peeple rush in to grab the injured as saviours of rescue...
somewhere, urgent conclaves set up,
to settle the war on bargained peace...
somewhere people stand and hug the tree,
not allowing it to be cut, not allowing the hill to be razed...
somewhere governments act, put the leash on corporate greed,
somewhere in Norwegian Labs, a seed bank is set up
to save earth if it grows sans vegetation,
Somewhere scientists work on exploring an alternate earth...
Somewhere on riverbanks and ponds, frogs croak and croak,
poets, thinkers, writers, humanists, raise voice for good sense to prevail...
Somewhere kindness oozes and drips, when they at warfront,
stop it for a day, hug each other
extending greetings of the special day...
Hope not a far cry... the thunder and darkness
the precursor of an enlivening rain about to fall...

©® **Molly Joseph**

HOPE

BHAGIRATH CHOUDHARI, India

Hope is the breath of life
Makes man to rise above
Existential squalor and strife
Hope motivates man
Making man to dare
For subduing anxiety and despair
Hope makes man to dream
Invites and invokes man
To swim against the stream Hope is manna of mind
Making a man happy and kind
Evolution seeks to enlarge heart through hope
Inviting man
To climb and conquer life's mountain top
With hope and perseverance
Man can cross the abyss of
dark ignorance
Hope is the seed of imagination
Which keeps alive human creative passion
For building the mighty human nation
Imagination flies upon the wings of hope
Rising to higher altitudes of evolutionary human scope
Evolution breeds hope through reproductive Genetics
Human child becomes more than animal by Epigenetics
Human child is the hope of humanity
Who brings down upon earth hope and charity.

©® **Bhagirath Choudhari**

HOPE
Amb. PRIYANKA NEOGI, India

By keeping in the night to sleep, hopefully.
The dream of the new dawn is lost in the distant border,
The smell of the poet's pen in the rural poet, the rhythm smiles.
Become the jolt of the light by pouring the light in the dark,
In an endless painted dream, in the dream,
Hope to "trust" to create life.
The sunshine becomes sweet in the sweetness of the sweetness,
Attracted to the aroma of winning with the storm,
Day after day, :the war to survive" in preparation.
Hopefully "encouraged and inspired",
"The dream keeps the dream, saved, stubbornness,
Gives a thousand ways to win the war of life".
Keeps hungry, saved love,
Keeps the imagination of winning life.
"Assurance power and desire".
"There is color in life" in the hope
The colorful vales check the excellence,
Slopes the stir in the mind of the mind,
"Hope is a reflection of light in life".

©® **Priyanka Neogi**

YOU ARE LIKE...

SANKHA RANJAN PATRA, India

You are like sunshine ,
You are like rain,
So pretty, so pure
So, I am without pain.
You are like Ocean,
You are like heaven,
So wide and so wise
So, I am without pain.
you are like a red rose,
As fresh as a new dawn,
You are like a sweet scent
As fresh as a bright morn.
You are like a cascade
As fresh as sunbeams,
You are like a rivulet
As fresh as moonbeams.

©® **Sankha Ranjan Patra**

OUR GOD – OUR HOPE

ASHOK CHAKRAVARTHY THOLANA, India

When clouded by uncertainty
One finds no one in proximity;
Hope alone boosts confidence,
Stands firmly in heart's presence.
The fear that grips and surrounds
There often isolation resounds,
But God appears as the real hope,
Certainly, all our worries stop.
When gloom spreads ominously
And anxiety surfaces ferociously,
The Almighty gives real boost,
Under His care, it's a real treat.
As and when the advancing age
Unbridle its inevitable rage;
We cannot leave it to our fate,
Hopeful God can only motivate.

©® **AshokChakravarthyTholana**

THE POWER OF HOPE

Dr. KANWALPREET BAIDWAN, India

Hope is a mighty word, not just four letters put together,
It has the strength to light up the most disheartened mind,
It acts that ray of sunlight, that filters into a room,
Through a tiny crack, lighting up a sad soul,
To gear up for a fresh start, it becomes the reason to try just once more,
The consecutive, successive falls, are alarmingly discouraging,
But it is hope that does not let one give up, and motivates for a better morrow,
Or get ready for another round of innings, the fear of failure is then dimmed,
Because one just hopes, it is a thought that gives shape,
To dream yet another dream, to sing yet another happy song,
To aspire, prespire and emerge victorious,
It is hope that makes one yearn for better days,
Despite the tests, the turmoil, and the various challenges.

©® **Kanwalpreet Baidwan**

WINGS OF HOPE

GARGI SIDANA, India

A rectangular mass perched over the shoulder to feel the lullaby of desire. Desire to blend
authentic taste of integrity and subtle connection.
Like a phoenix, its golden wings touch the profound layers of the dystopian world.
Like a lotus, fingers crossed, their legs nurture a breath of lucidity.
Like a crystalline luna, it woo the grey silhouette to sentient liberty.
Hope is an hourglass lying between rage and humans to mold into water. Water of tranquil ocean
submerging in the obesity of translucency.
Hope is an orange circle bestowing a violet chance of survival. Survive to dream, conquer, and
rejoice.

©® **Gargi Sidana**

HOPE

Dr. PERWAIZ SHAHARYAR, India

The world rests on hopes and expectations
Homosapiens have been growing in the true relations
Where there is no hope and desire at all
Living organisms convert into rocks and dissertations
Hope can raise you from the dirty mud
Hope can bloom flower from a tiny bud
Hope and faith are the powerful luck
Which brings crown to king diamond stud
If you are in trouble and in stress
Don't stop achieving your target progress
Hopes and despair are natural phenomena
Like sun and shadow never regress
Among fires, smokes and smells of burning flesh
Humanity has lost dignity between ego clash
Let's HOPE, God will restore the peace
When civilians are dying, PRESS unable to flash

©® **Perwaiz Shaharyar**

HARVEST SEASON   **Dr. RAKESH CHANDRA, India**

This is a season of harvesting happiness
And joys after a long wait; It ends
The period of hard work, and signifies
The importance of human resilience and
Iron will, to face rough weather;
Though harvesting is an assured
phenomenon,
Once the seeds are sown or saplings
Find refuge inside the muddy field, yet
It doesn't happen sometimes when
A natural calamity totally uproots the
dreams
Of the cultivators, so meticulously conjured
Up during the growth of crops; sometimes
Dreams turn into daydreams without giving
A hint even;
Harvest season enhances the camaraderie
Among the people for some time; everybody
Seens to enjoy the symphony of music
divine;
In the atmosphere filled with mirth and
humour,
Who would not aspire to dance in gay
abandon?
In the harvest season, the hardworking
Individuals are paid back handsomely
By the nature and Almighty; It also augurs
An era of repeating the same exercise
With equal zeal and enthusiasm in all
The circumstances;
Harvest season symbolizes the spirit
Of Resurrection, and inspires
Human beings march ahead in life With
equanimity.

©® **Rakesh Chandra**

THE HOPE   **RAJASHREE MOHAPATRA, India**

Hope, that hints existence of light
In the pitch-black darkness around
And is the spirit within the self that keeps
One alive in the darkest hours of a prolonged night.
Hopes mend our broken heart
While allowing drops of tear to roll down as Gentle rain , that cleans the stiches of
Torn heart washing away our pain and strain.
Hope, removes fear of mind
Against haunting echoes of thoughts
And eroding intimidations of any kind.
Hope flows in silent
streams assimilating
Shattered dreams , preserving it as
Starred memory of troubled past .
One has to learn to heal and cherish by self
under the canopy of hope in the darkest of the night.

©® **Rajashree Mohapatra**

BEYOND THE BONDAGE   **ASOK DAS, India**

Now make myself free,
9 AM in a bondage, stuck to it
For many a year-
Stuck to the Name- Fame- Game
Day in and out to face a crowd
from morn to night,
All come to ask something
Carrying painladen hearts.
As if all are running from one room
To another, to get a handful of
Freedom.
Now make myself free…
Open the doorstopper
I would mingle in the cluster of cloud
In the free sky
I would rent a house thereby
Please, make myself free,
For ever.

©® **Asok Das**

A HOPE TO RISE

The glorious sun is set
But a hope to rise again is left.
There is no use to lament
For the vanishing sun
Or the passing moon crescent.
The world will bathe again
In the saffron sunlight
After a dark and gloomy night.
Coming and going, arrival and departure
Are the predestined steps of divine procedure.
The Sun may set but the glory will shine
Dipping into the mystic river divine.

©® **Zainul Husain**

Dr. ZAINUL HUSAIN, India

HOPE

The embryo is in womb of mom.
It's the life's ever-beginning-home.
It's the hope of the life's flow.
Hope of the common breathing blow.
Child and mom, both are only one.
Times run and run...
Hope reaches to the ultimate destination.
Birth of the baby is the absolute creation.
This new life is the hope of the entire universe.
This hope is the most powerful binding of us.
This hope is continuing for endless time.
This hope is the creature's prime.
Every life is exist only for the hope.
Let's look at the Moon and realise the ever-hope.
From the next night of the New Moon night,
The hope makes the thin Moon as full Moon,
with light.

©® **Anjali Denandee, Mom**

ANJALI DENANDEE, MOM, India

HOPE **BALACHANDRAN NAIR, India**

Sporting a deceitful smile, peeping out of safron silk wrap,
SUN climbed down the train at destination East
Acknowledging chirping of birds and bang of temple bells
He pumped life to another day of exceptional hopes.
HE tied silver anklet on dancing waves' ankles.
Distributed sumptuous recipes to hungry green leaves
Applied varying colors on petals of blossoming buds
Reserved colour black for all those outlived alloted time.
HE gave freedom to man to call him God or Demon
Man, misusing that freedom, cut, held little bit of Sun
In packets, pockets, cells and in shelves, moving or stagnant
Sun, still shining heavy plum, hung pointed at man's pate!
The anklets on waves broke splattered on rocks
Leaves folded hands, bent head tired and slept
Man prayed for darkness to rest and enliven another day's hopes
The Hope, sheer black in colour out of galvanoscope!

©® **Balachandran Nair**

FORTRESS OF HOPE

ABEERA MIRZA, India

What is it that makes me different from the rest?
I would have to say it's the fact that I've passed every single test.
Each day I make sure my depression knows it's in a fight,
I jab with the left and follow through with the right.
Happiness is not a given, I know it must be earned,
Success awaits me if I want it, this chance must not be spurned.
At times I truly struggle and I morph into warrior mode,
I am battle hardened and I live life by a certain code.
I must lead by example and look after myself,
This is instrumental in conquering my mental health
It's nonnegotiable, I will never quit,
This attitude is the reason why I'm mentally fit.
I'm hungry for success, I have an unquenchable thirst,
When I battle my depression, I make sure I come first.
That's a lot to deal with but I manage to cope,
My mind is a fortress, I create my own hope.

©® **Abeera Mirza**

HOPE'S EYE   **MD EJAJ AHAMED, India**

Hope arises in your eastern horizon as the morning star.
When you are wrapped with blanket of fog by despair.
Fog goes away slowly, and your blue earth becomes brighter.
She stands by you like a loving mother,
She acts as a motivational speaker,
She helps to start new lives,
She makes photosynthesis in your mind's leaves,
Her eye shows your dreams,
In the evening sky as the evening star her eye arises.

©® **Md Ejaj Ahamed**

WHEN DREAMS TURN IN TO NIGHTMARES

PRIYATOSH DAS, India

When dreams turn in to nightmares
When hope run after mirage
When the wheels of life derail from the track.
With catastrophic pains in the deep heart's core
When the Titanic of hopes and aspirations
Sinks in the bottomless sea,
When the scorching Sun dries up the ocean-
When the soul- mate burries in to the graveyard...
When endeared mother,when the beloved father leave us following the rules of life,
The efulging fire
Burn them in to ashes of the pyre
When nurtured flowers are destroyed in the calamitous storm;
When no one is left to-
 partake of sorrows and pains
When no one is left to share pleasurable days of blissful spring
When no is one left to sing in unison and accompany the adventurous journey of the life
When excruciating pains of
separation break heart
Must not we lose hope with sadness O! the dispirited souls
We must continue our untirring efforts facing with all odds of life with undaunted spirit and determination ,
To achieve cherished mission of life
Vowing down head to the sublime feet of the Omnipotent God
Who is omnipresent in the midst of us-
He will guide us to reach our goal
 For he is the mightiest magician
He has the charismatic power and panacea to heal our wounds to regain lost beauty of life and usher a new dawn.

©® **Priyatosh Das**

HOPE IS LIFE   **Prof. Dr. LAXMIKANTA DASH, India**

Life engulfs with hope
Hope begets aspiration shop
Aspiration sprouts happiness
Happiness abdicates all darkness.
Hope energies life to sustain in the earth
It moulds negativity into positive mathe
Hope inspires life to go further
It germinates urge towards sanguine behaviour.
Hope builds the tower of returns in a few moment
It also gives sadness of devident
Where there is hope, there is pain
Abolition of hope makes life propitious gain.
Existence of life stays on hope
Too much hope makes a wide gap
Doing duty with positive approach makes life hopeful
Hope gives happiness to life silently for beautiful.

©® **Laxmikanta Dash**

HOPE

SUDIPTA MISHRA, India

The boatman moves on
towards an unknown destination
With a rowing oar
he drifts along
The sea,
a melting point
of thousands desires
embraces everyone
The horizon reflects
the dusky region of the sky
My emotions multiply
in this cosmic celebration
I know
in my eyes
dreams soar high
Like the loud waves
Of this silent sea
know not
where is my next direction
Let me come along
with the flowing wind
of this sea
This oar of the boatman
Alone knows
to tear the chest of the vast sea
for the voyage
of my hidden dreams

©® **Sudipta Mishra**

HOPE

SHIKDAR MOHAMMED KIBRIAH, Bangladesh

Spirit of Sensitivity
Optimism! Life-pulse of existence
A spirit of constant creativity
Highway to self-realization.
Pessimism! A self-aware suicide
Immersed in abyss of inactivity
A non-existence of God!
Dwelling in the optimism
Is the vital consciousness
Of existence that guards
Breaking down from vain
Moves to facing aversion
And promotes civilization
In the desired avenue of
Stability and prosperity.
Hope is the spirit we must need
That refills us with lively speed.

©® **Shikdar Mohammed Kibriah**

REGARDING HOPE

RANA ZAMAN, Bangladesh

Waiting for hope is positive aspect
Hope is nothing but a special tact
Enthusiasm takes the hope forward
Noble thought set frees captive bird
Willingness tends to implement hope
Irrational hope noose around the neck
Let the willingness climb up the rope
Laden people falling fail pull him back
Try and try again try to reach the goal
Hard nut to crack is nothing gather coal
Eradicating all evils hope start to foal
Rumblings might be malign to dream
Iodoform applying will act more better
Gyration may be need to weed's trim
Hallelujahs will be blessing against hater.

©® **Rana Zaman**

HOPE

S AFROSE, Bangladesh

This is omnipotent for all
Hope is the core at any role
Be yourself be the best
Face the rest with winning crest.
Nothing is easy to catch
Though you have made the prospect
So many times mind-set
Finally the traumatic vest.
Look at there the sunshine
Calls you for new rhyme
Can't you catch this moment?
Hope is the pedestal for each stage.

©® **S Afrose**

HOPE FOR STAYING ALIVE

With the colour of our eyes
Life begins and ends with hope.
Cloudy day ends with a smile of sunshine.
We stay alive with the hopes—
The powerful emotional act.
The guiding light propelling forward
Offering belief in better future.
That wishful thinking actively empowers
in our goals of success.
Hope leads aspirations to the best destiny.
In adverse situations of life
It's the active force of motivation.
Only hopes can make us stand for
our dreams of expectation and happiness.
Creating all the positive changes within us
And the world around human beings.

©® **Sayeeda Aziz Chowdhury**

SAYEEDA AZIZ CHOWDHURY, Bangladesh

MYSTIC PENCIL

NILOY RAFIQ, Bangladesh

On the hills of moonlight, blooms of the mind have fallen,
A self-destructive net drifts in the stream of regulated time.
No one has come to the echoing field of shadow,
Where the boat of clouds sank in the depths of water.
Glowing eyes flicker, beckoning in silent signals, A pure diver searches the ocean of creation,
And on that distant shore, a dead rose floats to the surfaces.
In the gathering of flowers, a blunt-lipped river,
The drowning bird takes flight into the endless sky.

©® **Niloy Rafiq**

MY LAST RESORT HOPE

TAPAS DEY, Bangladesh

The sky is overcast,
It doesn't mean the forecast of rain,
It is an arcanum of wailful tears,
An unspoken agony of the days,
For losing all cherished dreams.
I'm dumbstruck!
Always a smell of war is a panic,
To the commoners across the world.
Who cares for life and death,
Only the dance of prowess in the front,
Shouting,' Kill and get killed.'
Yet, my last resort is HOPE.
I'll see the little children flying,
Colourful kites in the blue sky,
Living in a floral and peaceful society.

©® **Tapas Dey**

HOPE: MELODY OF THE GOOD DAY

AKLIMA ANKHI, Bangladesh

Hope the star of dark night.
Messenger of shiny day.
Hope the rain drop, the fallen Bakul.
Life of dry earth, the garland's flowers.
Hope the fragrance of musk in the wood of fear
Hope the thunder of cloudy day.
The happiness of bee in the flower garden.
The union of love pollen in the cropland.
Hope is the Apple seed.
The secret plan of the good day.

©® **AKLIMA Ankhi**

HOPE

ALAM MAHBUB, Bangladesh

Hope has a beginning,
 it doesn't never be end
The emptiness is covered
in the inner story
But still hope remains alive.
Even in the sun-colored rain,
Everyone just acts by shaking the stage
And sighs also arise
On the yellow leaves of life
The shadow of hope breaks the circle of hard earth.
Life continues like a flowing river
From sky to sky, from desert to desert
With a procession of light
Only the roots remain alive in hope
And the people also live in coloring dreams of hope.

©® **Alam Mahbub**

HOPE

SANTOSH KUMAR POKHAREL, Nepal

Hope descends from the sky
and nestles in the heart.
The mind remains unaware —
busy weaving endless arguments
That lead to nowhere.
There are no ways.
So I've stopped questioning my mind
these days.
Hope sits in the heart, then swells in the eyes.
Tears begin to fall,
and the heart twists.
Look! Again, the heart starts wrenching.
Hope flew toward the sky
as I called out to her.
A bomb exploded in a distant land,
again, lives were lost.
Stop bombing!
The noise deafens me.
I looked up at the sky
Hope was still gazing down
from above.

©® **Santosh Kumar Pokharel**

HOPE AS HUGE SOURCE OF SURVIVAL

TIL KUMARI SHARMA, Nepal

The huge expectation of life is sense of hope.
Otherwise, we can not survive.
The sense of hope changes the lifelong survival.
It brings the positive mind of life.
It is the PowerPoint of living status.
Hope heals huge disease.
It builds the home of existence.
It brings the might of life.
Hope is the strong home of the people.
It brings the sense of healthy mind.
It is the huge respect of life.
Bring hope when you are hopeless.
Even death seems lower in front of hope.
So, hope is higher than death.
Hope provides success of every dreams.
It heals the depressive mind.

©® **Til Kumari Sharma**

DESIRE TO LIVE

RENUKA BHATTA, Nepal

Pushing the time one stride backward
And claiming to move forward
leaving the wind back
Where is human heading?
Restricting himself inside home
poor human says-
"We can't contact eyes
with atrocious Mr. Death
roaming around our home".

©® **Renuka Bhatta**

HOPE

ANGELA CHRONOPOULOU, Greece

Drizzles of sadness soak our Hope.
Our life is an indefinite postponement:
drops of joy in oceans of loneliness.
Unfairly.
That Tomorrow was not to come.
As you said: Hope is a pill.
Resignation is redemption.
An inevitable landing.
The bitter taste of Calmness.
Not to wait for anything.
Even this, is a victory...

©® **Angela Chronopoulou**

HOPE

EFTICHIA KAPARDELI, Greece

**The guards spent around the Sun
and spring who never woke
Hope full of ornaments
resides in all sites
I wake a day decision
eternity of loneliness
The Colours look really in
in the wall of dream
with fire bright red roses
the wings of birds
in the middle of the world
with her
I will leave**

©® **Eftichia Kapardeli**

HOPE FOR LIFE

CHRISTOS DIKBASANIS, Greece

I have built my new colony
deep in the celestial abyss
I made her strong, to withstand the merciless time
Upon it may bloom desires for the future
It is my only possession
that I stole from the First Creatures
I don't know if my mind can withstand
so much purity,
so much wealth of emotions,
so many fertile destinations,
so much primordial, sparkling essence of soul,
so much bread and wine of unspent youth,
so many vows to my Creator,
its sacred fire burning eternally within my heart
However, I expect
to acquire the glittering wings of an eagle
just before I breathe my last breath,
to rise to the bright horizons of new worlds
where I will live my most imperishable dreams,
acquiring an immortal body and spirit unharmed
by the deceptive, seductive desire
for perishable and soul-destroying things,
to become an eternal flower of a life within hope

©® **Christos Dikbasanis**

HOPE

Sunny joy
compositions
a collection of bright feelings…
Tired soul
laden with pains
under the snow
silence of the one
fight for survival…
The dream rises…
lyrics…
goals and visions lie
on the shoulders of thought
Euphoria of peace
in the blooming gardens
of the heart upon arrival
of a new promising ….
of sunny hope!

©® **Petros Kyriakou Veloudas**

**PETROS KYRIAKOU VELOUDAS,
Greece**

HOPE

XRYSOULA FOUFA, Greece

Hedges of hawthorn
hugged the roses
loneliness penetrated the garden.
Little branches crushed on soil
void of life.
No birds around.
A seed of emptiness
covered the space
turning our love into a ghost
haunting the tale.
Oh, dear,
come back to me again!
I plead you!
Look at my sorrowful eyes
and fill my heart with hope again.
I beg you, my only love!

©® **Xrysoula Foufa**

I TOLD YOU, HOPE

Centuries-old ices are melting.
It was cold and anxious in the hearts.
Endless hopes are here today.
But do we see further than the memory.
What will wake you from your sleep
Touched by deceitful idols.
Man, is the world yours.
Or the hopes are memories.
Centuries of sins are melting away.
Awakened souls build Earth.
And you walk with the scepter of your burden.
And you repeat again: – I told you, didn't I?

©® **Rozalia Aleksandrova**

ROZALIA ALEKSANDROVA,
Bulgaria

THE HOPE   **ZLATINA SADRAZANOVA, Bulgaria**

A morning full of hope.
The hope is a symbol of love.
And the happiness quietly appears.
Happiness is to wake up alive
and kicking.
Happiness is to have somebody to share hard and good days with.
Happiness is to have somebody to tell how your day was.
Because somewhere somebody carries you within themselves.
Happiness is to love and to be loved.
Give smiles, love, kindness and hope.
We are what we leave behind.
Every time when we touch somebody's heart or somebody's life,
the world changes because we give a piece of ourselves.
We live with faith, love and hope.

©® **Zlatina Sadrazanova**

SHADOW OF HOPE

NATALIJA NEDYALKOVA, Bulgaria

With time you learn
to love even the bad weather
to hear the silence
to be silent on a hundred languages
even those that
nobody speaks anymore
you understand that you are a shadow
of your own shadow
it is a play of light,
you are a reflection
of hope.

©® **Natalija Nedyalkova**

HOPE

NADYA RAYKOVA, Bulgaria

Your eyes -
Of an angel,
They open the heavens.
With your lashes
you scatter all the dark clouds
over the world.
Holy Love is beaming
from your irises.
It is refracting.
In my heart.
And spreads across Earth
To tell that you exist.
That you are here
and from today, until my last living cell
My name is
Hope

©® **Nadya Raykova**

CREATING HOPE **YORDANKA GETSOVA, Bulgaria**

Hold on, my dear friend.
This is a test like no other.
Hold on –
But not with your hands; strength is not what's needed.
Lock your gaze with mine – I won't let go,
even when the ground disappears beneath us.
Hold on – your heart to mine, soul to soul,
your promise to mine, word to word.
What will it cost us, and how will we pay?
No, not in silver or gold – that means nothing.
You and I, we create. We shape.
No one else will understand.
Our prayers will rise – longing, fierce –
to the farthest reaches of the Universe,
carried by Love –
never doubt it.

©® **Yordanka Getsova**

HOPE   **TSVETA MIHAYLOVA, Bulgaria**

The world around me chokes on hidden base and hate,
a secret venom sealing every fate.
And I - a forgotten cosmos, lonely and unseen -
long to preserve the dream that lies between.
Long ago, life struck us like a winter's bitter blast,
a force so fierce its chill was meant to last.
And in the quiet of this secret night I spread
a handful of beloved buds, tenderly shed.
Patiently I nurtured them from prying, hateful eyes,
shielding each fragile bloom from unkind despise.
I tremble with true hope, pure and burning bright,
for light to follow after every endless night.

©® **Tsveta Mihaylova**

HOPE

KIEU BICH HAU, Vietnam

We know we are poets
Our words are pearls
Some people think they are poets
But they play with words and human fate, then break them
Some people respect us
Most people think we are crazy
But we know we are poets only
We are not politicians
We do not care about earning an income or status
But we know about caring for another soul
We know how to stay true to ourselves
We do not try and reach the top
But we meet our needs in life
We travel around the world, carrying only 23 gram of being
We heal them, let them fly and sing
We know how to treat mental disorders
Our hearts are the unlimited banks of love
We are poets
We are soul savers who bring hopes
We have seen poverty and abundance
We have seen suffering and greed
We have seen love and hate
They are all different accounts
And they can withdraw from our hearts some poems to feed their days…

©® **Kieu Bich Hau**

HOPE IN MARCH   **VAN DIEN, Vietnam**

Every March, the Red River looks clear,
Shad swim upstream, spawning near.
You and I, on the dike so high,
Wind whispers songs as dragons fly.
Bamboo rows sway, shielding the tide,
Starlings chirp, calling far and wide.
A plump spider, gleaming bright,
Lilies bloom, a garden's delight.
Early sun makes leaves sway and swoon,
Longans cradle young fruits in June.
Wild orchids once just sprouting shy,
Now in full bloom, reaching the sky.
March brings hope, life anew,
Bridging earth and heaven the same light.
Who named this time *Thanh Minh* bright,
For hearts to seek their roots in mind?
To find again my childhood's grace,
March, oh March — hope's embrace.

©® **Van Dien**

HOPE

LE DUYEN, Vietnam

Wish to break and open the asylum's door,
To bring you home to a bright new shore.
The path of happiness we longed to see,
Together, our love will soar endlessly.
The ice within will soon melt away,
From stones and dust, love finds its way.
Erasing the years of loneliness and pain,
Fools in this world, yet love keeps us sane.
In life's inn, with no wealth or gold,
We live in silence, in deep shadows.
Yet love's desire stands strong and true,
A guiding flame, forever in view.
Wait for me, let's step toward tomorrow,
Though struggles may stretch, lined with sorrow.
The dream-filled sky we've always known,
Hope remains, forever being together.

©® **Le Duyen**

HOPE   **HONG NGOC CHAU, Vietnam**

In life, there are many vicissitudes, indeed.
Faith and hope that everyone needs.
Is a state of mental excitement, I think,
Boundless source of power overflowing
Storms and tempests do not fall really
Pain and overcoming all difficulties
Our future steadily searches, in action
Humanism spreads in all directions
Hope is always a flame, as ever
This world's passionate desire
Escape for the weary soul, day by day
Keeping faith and hope day by day
For yourself and spread it everywhere, hope
For the world to be filled with warm love
Create the most positive wave, I think
Like the sun of truth spreading

©® **Hong Ngoc Chau**

HOPE

Hope in the air, a smell of death trying.
World — a frightened child, clouds their view.
Dusty — there's no breath, life is forest.
Scaring, wild steps are lonely, with no sound.
Who can hear them? You can see with...
His knees on the ground — every man is.
Meant to be — this journey, a dangerous road.
Are you ready for its ghost? If you are,
Take out your sword — if you're weak,
You'll be lost. Your destiny is written.
Down from this point, there's no bad.
Mother Earth, like a clown, waters dirty.
Grass is black — but you're not lonely.
This war — you must fight all your fears.
The sky will open, every pore.
To embrace all your tears — pray in wait.
For the call — hope and faith, you must.
Have salvation — is near, break the wall.
God loves us — we'll be saved.

Ana Stjelja (Ana S. Gad)

Dr. ANA STJELJA, (ANA S. GAD), Serbia

PARALLEL WORLD   **TANJA AJTIĆ, Serbia/Canada**

Maybe I'm happy in a parallel world,
and maybe I'm beautiful and don't even know it?
Maybe there I breathe,
because here it's not like that,
here only the air passes
in exhale and sigh,
with mere survival
of a difficult life.
While there, elsewhere,
I have a smile, and I don't think too much,
because I'm happy,
and there I'm not alone in the wilderness like here.
There, in the parallel world,
I am again
with hope.

©® **Tanja Ajtić**

HOPE

IRENA JOVANOVIĆ, Serbia

Hope is a beautiful flower of intention
that resonates with my secret desires
opening all doors to life fluidity
preparing my heart to bloom mildly
in the most amazing and rhapsodic way.
Mesmerized by hope's gentle touch
I elegantly spin with an elevated whirl twist
entering an entirely new dimension of joy
where hope becomes the most cherished reality
nurtured and celebrated opulently
while I dream about it, deeply, deeply.
Hope is developing my inner views
giving my essence a true mist of refinement
sparkling through microtubules of time
divine bliss and conuscious brilliance.
Hope is a nice tool for all souls awakening.

©® **Irena Jovanović**

HOPE

ZDENKO ĆURKOVIĆ, Croatia

In the depths of my blue - peace,
pure as a tear, like a child's soul,
I can hear him, even now the cricket is playing,
karst and stones; The High Sun burns - drought.
In the vastness of my universe,
Pure as the Blessed Virgin Mary,
I'm going to burn my breath - the light of peace.
And it will burn, as long as my sun shines.
In the depths of my star-studded battle,
as a source of life, as a source of water,
my mother's whistle is burning - the candle of serenity,
And it will burn, as long as my moon walks.
In the bliss of my heavenly infinity,
Pure as pure gold weaves light,
And my heart is on fire, and I am smiling.
And it will burn, as long as my star shines.

©® **Zdenko Ćurković**

HOPE

MARINA ŠUR PUHLOVSKI, Croatia

It is not true
that hope dies last.
Hope never dies,
that's why it is a hope,
but not hopelessness,
which exists
only in words.

©® **Marina Šur Puhlovski**

HOPE

DANIJELA ĆUK, Croatia

Hope always lives in us,
both when there is sunshine and when
there is darkness, it exists, it is there,
with us in good times and in bad.
Without hope,
It's as if we don't exist,
we live in a vortex of problems,
we don't see a way out, we fight in vain,
we fight hard battles in vain.
Do not lose hope, be hope too,
embrace the community of love,
every struggle is difficult, but you
should know this,
hope does not allow us to fall to the
bottom.

©® **Danijela Ćuk**

HOPE WITH ALL   **FROSINA TASEVSKA, Macedonia**

We navigate our lives through difficulties,
trials, pain, and various everyday cruelties,
all in pursuit of our dreams for a brighter day,
with the hope that all negativities will fade away.
Hope means believing in times of sorrow,
calming and envisioning a happier tomorrow.
It's the light at the end of the tunnel, the North Star,
offering guidance when we don't know where we are.
We should give thanks to God in all circumstances
whether bad or good
even when we feel misunderstood.
Instead of allowing ourselves to sit and mope,
we must take action, change our thoughts,
and always, always hold onto hope!

©® **Frosina Tasevska**

HOPE   **ELIZABETA DONČEVSKA-LUŠIN, Macedonia**

Once you told me
hope is in the stars above.
Do you know that even now,
after all this time
my eyes are still fixed upon the sky.
And I recognize them all .
The Ursa Major – the mighty Bear,
And the Ursa Minor – the smaller light,
the Sagittarius and Cassiopeia...
Just as you taught me!
And do you know that there is no such World
in which I look upon Stars
and do not see – You!
The Stars and me, are silently making
an exchange between the Worlds.
Constellation – for Man!

©® **Elizabeta Dončevska-Lušin**

HOPE DIES LAST　　　　　　　　　　**ČEDOMIR B. ŠOPKIĆ, Macedonia**

Ooo, wonderful hope, foundation, of earthly happiness,
heavenly gift, greater than the whole world, what without
what would we do without you, we sufferers
You are a little close to us, but still so far away,
my whole heart is with you
joy and wise thoughts you fulfill it for us.
We wish with hope, we live we also work we die
hoping for everything we believe and expand
with hope our joy is longer without seeking fame.
Ooo, lok easy, and seemingly heavy,
He smiles at us from heaven, awakens the best in man,
the elixir of life gives us, blessed are those
to whom hope is, the beginning and the end of each day.
Lift us, brave us optimism spreads,
it puts a halo on us of the light of life
to easily confuse goodness and beauty.

©® **Čedomir B. Šopkić**

HOPE

Today, you will leave far away
I will leave far too
everyone will be cocooned in their orbit
hope remains
that you will stray to the planet of our love
while I put together a mosaic about us
long-awakened butterflies in the stomach
I lock in my magic shell
we burn on the bonfire of love
shell, butterflies, and me
you shine with the brilliance of a thousand stars
over the planet, my darling
and you raise the hope of a new meeting
in some corner left for us

©® **Ibrahim Honjo**

IBRAHIM HONJO,
Bosnia and Herzegovina/Canada

HOPE

Even when the heart turns to stone
where sorrow lies locked away
sealed long ago,
a spark of hope still glimmers
like a newborn star
and like a whisper in the wind.
There still exists a spark of hope,
stronger than granite,
hope that shatters stone
and melts the hardest steel,
hope that will fill a wounded heart
and a lost soul
with humanity once more.

©® **Ensar Bukarić**
Translated by Haris Bukarić

ENSAR BUKARIĆ,
Bosnia and Herzegovina

HOPE WITHIN ME

Maybe I wrote to you on some distant night?
Maybe I spoke of rivers or oceans,
Of sorrowful dawns and endless longing?
I loved the moon, the power of its glow.
I counted the stars, gave each a name…
Wrote you poems and beautiful verses.
Wandered with the wind through desolate lands,
Gathering dreams that slipped through my hands.
And nothing remains in this very moment
When I realize I love only your shadow,
And where you are, I am never there…
Here, where I exist, you are just a shadow,
Fading away softly without a trace,
Erasing what was once called hope.

©® **Cvija Peranović Kojić**

**CVIJA PERANOVIĆ KOJIĆ,
Bosnia and Herzegovina/Austria**

HOPE   ALEKSANDRA VUJISIĆ, Montenegro

The flowers are dead in the vase
but I have no wish to throw them away.
Their new, miraculous flourishing
is what I call hope,
or are they here to stay that way?
The love is lost in the nonsense
of everyday life, worn out as an old coat.
Its new, miraculous, reappearance is
what I call hate,
rocking with menace this old boat.
But there is the shore not so far away,
or even a lighthouse and I think
I can cope -
for all of the lost love or broken wings
I only have a ray of hope.

©® **Aleksandra Vujisić**

HOPE

EWITH BAHAR, Indonesia

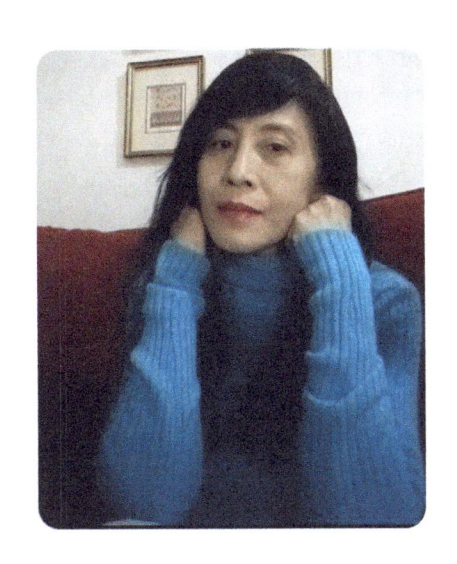

Life sometimes deceives, sometimes removes,
sometimes withdraws, sometimes mocks
And we face those challenges with strategy.
My unconquerable soul persists
in showing unwavering strength,
standing face to face with silent adversity
In weakness, we're blinded
But a best friend within, whispering reinforcement
Ignite the faint-burning light to be a flaming torch
A best friend within offers choices
to continue the journey
then we put the "giving up" button in the farthest distance
A best friend within…
It never leaves, yes hope never leaves.

©® Ewith Bahar

I HOPE YOU DON'T FORGET ME   WIRJA TAUFAN, Indonesia

I hope you don't forget me
Stay together every time
Reliving the memories in your arms
Like your shadow that always warms my soul
I looked into your eyes which then disappeared into the horizon
One distance out of thousands of miles hangs my hope
So far away, my days are turning arround
The remaining dust of the past covers my dreams and hopes
I try to be happy
Continue to be happy
Event if the day destroys my dreams, destroys my hopes
I hope my heartbeat will always vibrate in your soul

©® **Wirja Taufan**

O, HOPE

ERNESTO P. SANTIAGO, Philippines

I don't want to overdose myself
on failure in heart, twist and untwist.
Let the light from your eye of gist
see me for what and why I exist.
Like you, I am a waking dream
of tempting oracle stones, perceiving
to never stop in a pathway of believing
when waves of feeling are heaving.
Though love is my active choice,
when I am with you I am not fed up
with the rain, but hopeful not to give up
the sky with roses of pick-me-up.
Voices and words are willing
to come together, like red koi in the pond,
so we plunge not into a deep despond—
little fires of the heart respond.

©® **Ernesto P. Santiago**

HOPE'S GENTLE WHISPER

In the shadows where dreams may wane,
Where whispers of doubt so softly gain,
Hope's gentle whisper, a spark in the night,
Guides the weary through darkest plight.
When burdens heavy, hearts weighed down,
And life's cruel tempest wears the crown,
Lift your gaze to the horizon's gleam,
For hope endures in the darkest dream.
Through tears and trials, a fragile thread,
Hope weaves its light where fears have spread,
With every step, though paths unseen,
Hope's tender embrace, a soul serene.
Hold fast to hope, when times grow bleak,
In the depths of despair, its strength we seek,
For in life's trials, hope's light will ascend,
The beginning found where the endings blend.

©® **Marlon Salem Gruezo-Bondroff**

MARLON SALEM GRUEZO-BONDROFF, Philippines/USA

HOPE

RUT VARGAS-VIVAS, Colombia/USA

The beacon of hope illuminated the darkened forests, guiding the wandering sleepwalkers out of the lost abysses.
Their blind eyes sensed the glow amidst shadows and sunless horizons, and their pupils, mirrors without reflection, believed they glimpsed the gleam of an illusion.
A radiant glow pointed them the way, with its eternal, soothing light, and they awoke from their somber slumber to behold the promises of dawn.

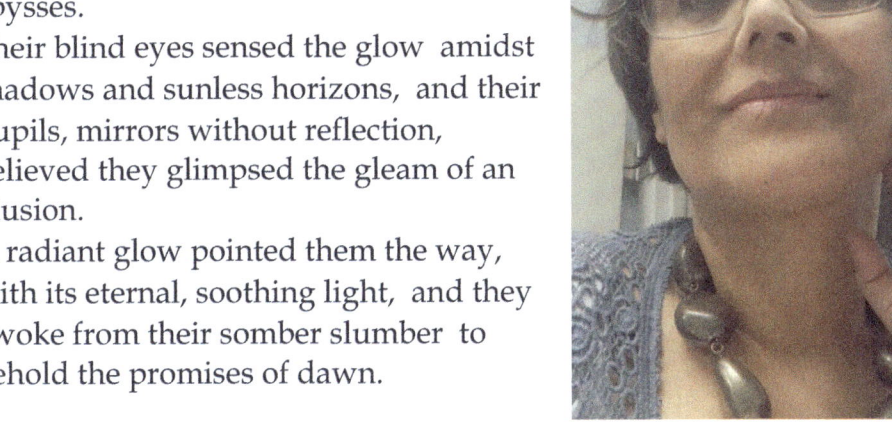

©® **Rut Vargas-Vivas**

HOPE

LASKIAF AMORTEGUI, Colombia

The green buds are in bloom.
They are the magic colour of hope.
The rainbow appeared in the sky.
At the end it has a treasure that guides the blind.
And gives them back their light.
Hope is impregnated with faith.
And pierces unknown dimensions.
It is the strength that lifts the warrior.
It is the energy that fuels people to endure any tragedy.
Hope smiles at us and encourages us to continue protecting mother earth.
It is similar to the breath that feeds us day by day to live.

©® **Laskiaf Amortegui**

A DROP OF HOPE

KUMARKHANOVA AINUR SERIKOVNA, Kazakhstan

A drop of hope appeared
Do not be silent? — In the heart from the chest;
I have - and how to forget you?
The heart pounded so frantically
What a miracle wanted to create.
I, Ainur, tell me, dear
What are the laws of life? Us
Give, Ainur you are fire to me
Do not find a source of trouble, but you know -
After all, Majnun will not come out of me.
He must get used to everything himself.
And the hopes of the banner are masking
We will cry with him together, we will squeeze
And let's go on the right path.
The mind will reveal the world of fantasies
to us!
Do not poke, love, heart in vain -
Let the natural world be transformed
That your unique image,
He sculpted from the mountains and rivers
with paradis,
Closing it with a sea wave.
But sparkling among the stars of heaven,
Create my good poet,
You are from life where you are not,
song for my soul…

©® **Kumarkhanova Ainur Serikovna**

HOPE

DINA ORAZ, Kazakhstan

When the heart freezes with pain,
The soul weeps in helplessness.
Hope is always the last to die
And never looks truth in the eye.
It gives strength and lifts the spirit,
Though there is no faith in the best
With the light of love it pierces the darkness of hearts,
With warmth comes the dawn.
In spite of the bitterest deceptions,
Betrayal, envy, lies
Hope nourishes and strengthens
Faith, love and dreams.
In hospital wards and on battlefields,
Hope lives in prayer.
As we wait and call upon the Creator,
Love and goodness will save the world.

©® **Dina Oraz**

HOPE

ELHAM HAMEDI, Iran/Italy

"Counting Women in the Mirrors"

In sleep,
Windows awaken the walls.
Mirrors count the women within themselves,
And once more, they plant suns inside.
In sleep,
Mirrors reflect the sky upon my cheeks.
When I feel the steps of sleep in my eyes,
The mirror is filled with the colorful footprints of women.

©® **Elham Hamedi**

REAL, GENUINE HOPE **FARZANEH DORRI, Iran/Denmark**

Real, genuine hope looks at chaos and hell
and looks it straight in the eye and hopes anyway.
Real, genuine hope is the gasoline that keeps us going,
even when the wheels are shaking.
It does not make us passive, but makes us act.
Real, genuine hope gives us the energy to take the next step,
when darkness is a concrete reality
when life is sometimes heavy and hard.
It is the driving force to navigate the darkness,
to reach the light.
The hope that the deprivations are useful,
so that there is still strength for another round.
The hope that it will have an end, so that we do not drown in discouragement and indifference.
The hope that we are part of a story that ends well.
Hope is the anchor that keeps us grounded in life
and doesn't let us drift away into worries.
Hope is actually an excellent strategy.
Let there be hope as long as there is life.

©® **Farzaneh Dorri**

HOW HUMBLE IN THE TALL TREES — SHOSHANA VEGH, Israel

I haven't met them yet.
How deep is the fjord?
I haven't gotten to the end of it yet.
How quiet the streets are,
I haven't walked all the places yet.
And if a little boy in the southern peninsula,
Hungry for a slice of bread,
or thirsty for water,
The earth will grow wheat,
And man will reap,
And there will be food and water as well.
But in the war,
There's no food,
There is no hope.
When man seeks justice,
It does not grow in a place
Where pride rules.
Let's be low,
Modest in our demands.
Only the trees are tall and proud,
And also remain silent.

©® **Shoshana Vegh**

SMILE   **HANITA ROZEN, Israel**

I'm tired of being sad
My pain and tears are upon me
Every time my spirit breathes black
My smile is so desperate
hidden between wrinkles of worry,
Even my words are lying down
in the slope of my throat
have difficulty routing their way up,
I wish I could banish the darkness
which takes over brave drops of light
Those who are trying to make their way
From chilling thoughts in a harsh reality,
Only then maybe, maybe
When the beats of hope will dare to echo
A new dawn will manage to hang
On the rays of a wounded sun
I will force my facial muscles to smile,
A tiny smile.

©® **Hanita Rozen**

HOPE   **ISAAC COHEN, Israel**

I heard voices of war.
I gave a baby a pot
Of flowers of hope.
His tears made
The flowers grow
And they covered the world.
Peace emerged.

©® **Isaac Cohen**

WHISPERS OF HOPE

As time renews the shadows,
the light rotates by the pomegranates,
the apples,
and the green walls of eternity emerge.
Then, my voice rises to the peaks,
to the mountains,
to the leafless stems that soon regain
the exuberance of their leaves
in a pure and renewed space.
Then, a seascape embraces the pink
luminosity, which extends into the
horizon
like a blue seagull.
And seeds of happiness ascend
in light and fragrant scents of hope.

Maria do Sameiro Barroso

HOPE

Hope is the only thing,
What does a person have,
The soul and the body remember
About that from century to century.
Everyone cherishes hope,
When she's gone,
When they're smoldering in sorrow
For many years now.
She comes by herself...
she lives in everyone.,
And if she's wandering,
it's probably from thirst.
It's familiar to humans
The power to believe in hope.
And therefore Go ahead towards
Open the doors to hope.

©® **Natalie Bisso**

Dr. MARIA DO SAMEIRO BARROSO, Portugal

DR.HC. NATALIE BISSO, Germany

PHOTONS OF HOPE   LEO ACOSTA, Nicaragua

There is always a sun shining
in a stellar system,
which, in its biochemical process
of continuous transformation,
unfolds its prism in photosynthesis,
and in the quantum dance of its rays
lays an amalgam
upon the surface's carpet,
leaving in its luminous trail
the latent vibration
of a perpetual sensation.
Threads of hope are woven
in shimmering colors,
even in adversity
and in the most inhospitable places.
And life sprouts and takes shape
in the depths.
It has not yet perished in the dark
infinity:
it lives in waiting,
in perpetual motion,
where the hidden defies the human gaze.

©® **Leo Acosta**

HOPE

CORINA JUNGHIATU, Romania

Hope has no body, only echo and absence,
a shadow of gold, a smoky path that dissolves into the void,
a footprint on the horizon's line,
for you never know if you are walking or dreaming.
Hope is light, a circle without a core,
a river that crosses the clay mountains of dreams.
Hope is our choice to believe that what does not exist can,
in some way, become real, in a game of illusions,
a game in which even Pandora's box opens with each wish,
and the demons hide beneath the cloak of promise.
From that ancient box, nothing remains but hope,
like a mirage that entices us through the abyss of our own madness,
a dream of a future that will never come,
yet, in every moment, becomes more real than ourselves.

©® **Corina Junghiatu**

HOPE

TETIANA HRYTSAN-CHONKA,
Ukraine

The honest cross of the holy movement
Came and took to judge.
For truth, or for the finger,
Pointing us the world in the world.
For just so – to find yourself,
Forcing us to create ourselves...
Hope will wrap a wonderful fest,
Foreseeing a holistic manifesto.
Hope in the holy power,
Go with good through the world, peace.
Hold onto the fulfillment of being.
As ancestors fulfilled in you.
We are left to love,
Let evil lose itself.
We will live in the world.
We are heavenly People on earth.
Fest – good; You – you.

©® **Tetiana Hrytsan-Chonka**

HOPE   **FOLAJIMI NOTCH SHOAGA, Nigeria**

The seasons passes by expressing naturalness.
As expectation of mankind lies in life view,
Hope of survival sounds intrinsically in sense.
As literature beauty of life is a consolation in lieu.
Tending of life goals might have encountered miasma.
Gathering one's life together is a priority to win life dilemma,
Meanwhile, at a point may be a safer harbour closed to
The tendency mustn't be lost so as to achieve according to.
True literature life never tells human when's or why.
Reality of life journey never halt to correct mistakes,
Therefore, achieving greater height lies in hope
According to human nature and how would-be rely.
As a sane life literature as human characters
Comprehending life comprehensiveness is about being focus,
Mind wandering is as victim of illusion of nectars.
Therefore, faith and deeds is a strength of hope in locus.

©® **Folajimi Notch Shoaga**

A LIGHT OF HOPE

NORMA MARINA SOLIS ZAVALA, Peru

A ray of light pierced my soul
submerged in darkness
with thoughts of death,
pain and fear.
Thousands of voices in unison shouted
crying for justice,
asking for help
wrapped in seas of blood.
A terrifying image of human violence
that hits my spirit hard,
my tears fall and my heart explodes…
Until when will hatred continue to claim lives!
That light that illuminated the darkness
embraces my being with its warmth,
hope blooms in me again
maybe tomorrow this war will end.

©® **Norma Marina Solis Zavala**

HOPE

SANDRINE DAVIN, France

In the dark
Winter
The stars are going out
One by one
Sparrows on the edge
Electric
Rub their wings
Meanwhile
Spring
On the bench
An old man hopes
The return of his wife
Here
The stars
Make dreams come true

©® **Sandrine Davin**

ON HOPE

Ph.Dr. MA YONGBO, China

The so-called hope is false, like the landscape in the glass
this is not merely a matter of metaphor.
The rain falls, the rain keeps falling,
this is a fact. The rain turns the garden into a garden in the rain—
fountain, marble dome, statues, and lawn,
and through the glass windows—
blurry patches of color: trees, flowers, and birds.
One who gazes too long from the window
can hardly leave his chair.
Among the things around him,
there must be something eternal,
otherwise, we wouldn't live so long—
almost like Homer in his old age,
draining the sea, the sunset,
and the song of the sirens with a single word.
And what we commonly call hope
is a clumsy nanny leading us backward,
falling on the threshold,
her white apron splashed with flowers, opening,
let us unintentionally glimpse the goat's thigh.
Perhaps, we have always cried in repression,
and have finally been led into a garden transformed by rain,
where the bird's calls are hidden.

©® **Ma Yongbo**

BIRTH

ANNA MARIA MICKIEWICZ,
England

forgotten charm
neglected onion
and then a flower
a spring hope
first shoots
supposedly
we have no talent
supposedly
inspiration is born pure
uninvited
yet
it needs
a dust of burnt grass
of dried peat bogs
and suddenly
a bouquet
a tree
will bloom
a miracle

©® **Anna Maria Mickiewicz**

HOPE / PERMAFROST / PROJECTIONS

OLA GLUSTIKOVA, Slovakia

bear ointment / lynx tongue / boiled wolf hearts
musty legacies
in the first picture / grandma / in the middle /
herds of bison / the flock is watching / eyes
full of muddy water
in the next photo / my mom / ten years old / is posing
in hat and dress / white tights / next to her / a fawn /
a silent compound sentence / of the childhood
at another time / sister and me / buttercup yellow / rural
motives / apples greengages quinces / desires /
as lowlands in us / and the two of us / women
of the pine tree lineage / earth climbers / future
spacewomen / at sight full of / defiance water and resin

©® **Ola Glustikova**
Translated by M. Grmanová)

MY SPOILED ONE

YOUCEF MEBARKIA, Algeria

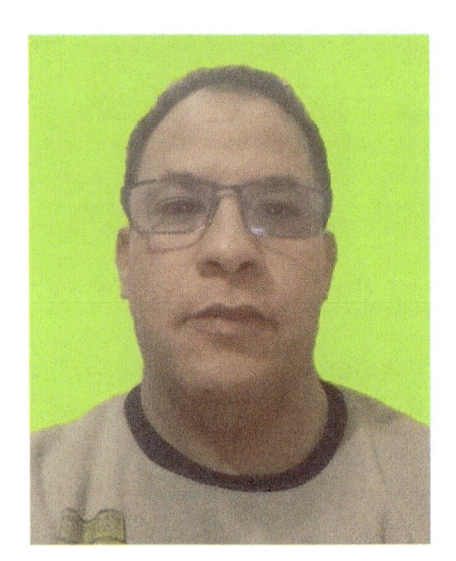

I drew you, my spoiled one
A bride in my imagination
Your white heart is beautiful
Innocent of my questioning
I try to curb my feelings
But I fail in my attempt
And every passionate person flees
Away from my fight
I argue on your behalf with my critics
And my opponent in my argument
And your pure heart knows
For sure the value of my status
I love you with a mad love
And I do not seek treatment

©® **Youcef Mebarkia**

HOPE

HUSSEIN HABASCH, Kurdistan

The woman hopes
to look beautiful in her own eyes.
The child hopes
to break his toys.
The homeless hopes
to find a shelter to sleep.
The drunkard hopes
to own a bottle of wine.
I hope to convince
the woman of her beauty,
the child to arrange his toys,
the homeless to find a shelter to sleep
and the drunkard to go to the bar.

©® **Hussein Habasch**

DOES THE EARTH HEAR ME?

GABRIEL S. WEAH, Liberia

Oh earth, where are your eyes and ears?
You have made me believe with enthusiasm,
You are everywhere, listening to my heart.
Now, broken like a mirror, I am in this world.
Sometimes, you made me feel like giving up.
When I think about my friend Hope, I just cry.
I wept not only because of my brokenness.
Look, many have died with frustrated tears.
Does the earth hear me?
I guess yes, but with deaf ears.
Impregnated is my stomach with sorrow.
When will you wash away my sour wine?
Earth, bleeding, is my dark continent.
You told me you are a virtuous woman.
When I look at you thoroughly, I see red oil.
Hope has failed me repeatedly; where are you, earth?

©® **Gabriel S. Weah**

MY HOPE AND FAITH IS IN THE LORD

DEBRA JOE, United Arab Emirates

The times my life has been like a roller coaster
with many ups and downs; I was stuck;
then I turned to my saviour;
I asked, I prayed and waited on Him,
He was and is my only hope
and yes my Lord blessed with what I had asked for,
he gave me strength to take life one day at a time,
as a widow he stood besides me
and I tell you just wait on him;
have faith and you will see the best of results.
I have asked and received!
My hope and faith is in the Lord alone!

©® **Debra Joe**

HOPE

NIKOLLË LOKA, Albania

For this God who became human!
Our mountains continue to grow,
and for a short time they will touch the sky,
they will carry there a stone and a little earth,
where God will swear:
For this stone that I carry on my back,
for this sky, mixed with the earth!
Our mountains continue to grow,
until God himself sits upon them,
then they will sit again,
and God will decrease.
Then people will swear:
For this God that I see with eyes!
and they will be healed.
Our mountains speak to God,
and his voice,
an echo comes to hearth.
We swear by His echo:
For this God who entered in house,
for this God who became human!

©® **Nikollë Loka**

HOPE SAJID HUSSAIN, Pakistan

Hope awakens as the life's first breath,
Illuminates the abyss of night with its golden discourse,
Ascending a celestial architect,
Orchestrates the stars in their cosmic ballet,
A silent ember ignites the infinite dusk,
An oracle of unseen horizon for contours of eternity,
It strides beside fate a sage of unseen pathways,
Weaving the fabric of existence with luminous threads,
Exhales within the dust of transience,
To compose symphonies in the silent currents of time,
Soul of hope flows as the river of resolve,
Inscribing its indelible decree upon the tides of destiny,
Hope inscribes the covenant of renewal upon the zephyr,
Pipe dream communes with the ocean's cadence,
It sways in philosophical reverence with the sentient trees,
Hope's ontological truth stands unshaken with an immutable force.

©® **Sajid Hussain**

HOPE

ELMAYA CABBAROVA, Azerbaijan

Hope ends in the end, everyone believes
They say that happiness awaits me.
Deceive yourself in the moonlight,
Wait for you in the lamp of hope.
Maybe one day the door will suddenly knock,
May your longing lover rejoice from the heart,
May the Creator have mercy on your tender bride,
Wait for you in the flow of years.
The horizon where the sun rises, in the dawn,
In the light of your eyes, in the rhythm of your heart,
In the last breath of the longing lover,
Hope awaits you with possibilities.
Tomorrow is unknown, mysterious,
And today awaits with hope, tomorrow,
Lovers, believers, oh, it is a prayer,
This colorful world awaits you.

©® **Elmaya Cabbarova**

Author of collage: Ljiljana Stjelja, Serbia

INTERVIEW

ROZALIA ALEKSANDROVA, Bulgaria   DINCHO CHOBANOV, Bulgaria

THE CHOSEN ONE-THE RELIABLE MESSENGER OF GOD

R Aleksandrova: - Please introduce yourself!
Dr. Dincho Chobanov: - I am the creator of the model and method LIGHTGRAM DIA TERRA (DIAGNOSTICS AND THERAPY through Lightgrams). I am the creator of the PRABOS system (PRABULGARIAN FIGHTING SYSTEM), I am the holder of a black belt, awarded personally by the doyen of martial arts in Bulgaria - Stefan Hinkov, for the theoretical and motor development of the system. I have published books in this connection: "PRABOS, THE KEY TO LONGEVITY" ,"PRABOS AND RHYTHMS" with a focus: the connection between the eastern symbolic system, Bulgarian folklore, bioenergetics, cosmic energy flow and health in all its forms and manifestations.

I graduated from the Technical University of Sofia with a degree in mechanical engineering. I also graduated from the National Sports Academy in Sofia. I am a martial arts trainer. At the New Bulgarian University I studied Stefan Hinkov's course on Asian symbolism. In addition to these qualifications, I have completed numerous internships and courses in martial arts and spiritual practices.

I actively practice LIGHTGRAM DIA TERRA, which includes spiritual and physical improvement,

R. Aleksandrova: - Could you describe the LIGHTGRAM DIA THERA method - what is it about?

Dr. Dincho Chobanov: - I accept the idea that Health is three-layered - physical, energetic, spiritual. In my opinion, the removal of any disease should go along this axis. For my work, I use Lightgrams - energy structures of my inner perception, which generate energy impulses.

The length of their wavelength depends on the type of Lightgrams. Thus, an electromagnetic field /EMF/ is formed around each Lightgram. I assume that the person is a Charge of this EMF. My diagnostics are based on an analysis of the interaction Electromagnetic Field - Charge. I find deviations from the ideal electromagnetic fields of each organ and system in our body. The subsequent bioenergetic balancing of these fluctuations is the main part of the LIGHTGRAM DIA TERRA method.

The spectrum of my developed sensitivity includes the detection of numerous pathogenic deviations such as: are there active or encapsulated infections in the body; toxins; metabolism; the reasons for difficult weight reduction; are there tissue changes in the body; what is mental health and its emotional state; which organs and systems are predisposed by inheritance to disease; is there an accumulation of harmful waves in the human body due to the presence of heavy metals and external fields; the functional waves of all internal systems and pathogenic symptoms due to their disturbed energy; what is the cellular potential, carrying information about the current and future health status, etc.

This same sensitivity gives me the opportunity to immerse myself in time and look into past and future events and facts. This helps to analyze the current situation and make decisions about our future activities.

I profess the idea of the limitless possibilities of bioenergy, of the electromagnetic properties of matter and light, and of movement as a source of EMF.

R. Aleksandrova: - Who is the predominant one in you: the healer, the scientist, the innovator, the teacher, the black belt holder, or... And where did it all start?

Dr. Dincho Chobanov: - Every person subconsciously feels their uniqueness. While he is young, he tries to find her. I also wanted to become different, visibly closer to God. I was fond of sports in all athletics disciplines, I defended my titles, I won competitions, but that was until the moment when martial arts entered my life more seriously. The impressive physical and energy techniques turned out to be the focus that I had dreamed of until then. I was one of the pioneers in Bulgaria who started classes in this direction. Student life in the capital Sofia helped me connect with many Asian masters. I attended many different trainings and internships with them. The fact of my personal acquaintance with Bulgarians dealing with philosophical movements from the East is also not without significance. Over the years, I practically realized their instructions and saw that energy is encoded in the symbols. My familiarity with the Asian "Book of Changes"/I Jing/ largely confirmed this hypothesis. This, on the one hand, complemented my esoteric understanding of Creation, and on the other, I accepted the idea that our thoughts can change reality. Years of hard work followed in the physical and energetic plane, an overview of many philosophical and esoteric theories about the mental and physiological processes inside and outside of us. This process was supplemented by training in scientific achievements in the field of quantum physics. In my searches, I clearly saw the connection between Eastern philosophy and Bulgarian folklore. I created a model. The structure of my model was supplemented and enriched at that moment when all my searches suddenly acquired divine expression. I received as a gift supersensitivity, which gave me the opportunity to see into the "invisible" – to connect with the universal energy wave, the timeline, to scan energy, mental and physiological states down to the cellular level, expressed through our quantum essence. And all this, regardless of distances, times, ages, gender, geographical location - a gift that is a responsibility and God's Blessing. Sensitivity, my engineering thought and knowledge of physics and mathematics allowed me to construct a healing system based on electromagnetic radiation - magnets, colors and spherical mirrors, imitating the solar system with its harmony and torsion fields. The construction successfully imitates the pyramidal structures and the essence of the mounds - i.e., their energy transforming power.

R Aleksandrova: - Can you describe how your gift works? Is there magic? How do you contact with the Universe?

Dr. Dincho Chobanov: - As I have already explained, my gift is connected with my internal electromagnetic radiation towards an object and subconsciously comparing its wavelength and frequency with mine. In this case, it is a standard. The degree of deviation gives me information about the health, time, space, etc. states. This is by no means an innate or acquired intuition, but the use of the informational universal field. Just as the Universe corresponds to a Higher Mind in order to be in balance and harmony, so my essence, as part of the universal, corresponds to this Mind.

R Aleksandrova: - What do you think is the place of the modern healer in our society?

Dr. Dincho Chobanov: - In my opinion, to be a healer, you need to have developed sensitivity and a lot of knowledge, that is, to be able to "see" the projections of the three types of human health - physical, energetic, spiritual. Each of them has its own laws relating to the structure, to a certain mechanism of connecting the details, to the function. The healer must have a good idea of the structure of Man - what we are, why we are what we are, what our mission is, how we fit into the universal model of creation, etc. A good healer must have his own treatment strategy and a comparative model for health levels. For this purpose, very deep knowledge, gift and dedication are required. Eastern models are good, but they are not presented in their entirety when training foreigners. They talk about the connection between the human physique, energy and spirit, but in my opinion not enough. Perhaps this is secret knowledge only for the inner schools and they zealously guard their centuries-old knowledge.

R Aleksandrova: - You shared that you are constantly receiving new models related to the Lightgram Dia Thera method, which you use in treatment and training? Would you open "The Door to your treasures" a little for our readers?

Dr. Dincho Chobanov: The acquired sensitivity gives me the opportunity to draw information from the "primary wave", in my opinion the wave from the primary cosmic explosion. It is the carrier of all information in the Universe. Time, spaces, dimensions are also encoded there. There is information about everything that is happening - upcoming, past events and facts, health, universal constructions. My sensitivity gives me the opportunity to immerse myself in this wave and draw information from it. Since my mission as a quantum healer is also related to training people, the way of projecting the "invisible" into the "visible" is through schemes, geometric symbols, colors, numbers, sound syllables, body positions. The information about their energy construction comes suddenly, as a general content, and my task is to construct the vision. It must have an energy balance, be consistent with the energy-information field, take into account time and the level of impact. In my collection "God the Beginning" I show in a simplified form my methodology of training in Lightgram Dia Tera.

R. Aleksandrova: - Do people who start to engage in spiritual cultivation and physical exercises according to your system at a, let's say, more mature age, have a chance to reach your level or at least a decent level?

Dr. Dincho Chobanov: - I have gone through a very difficult period in searching, comparing, practicing, accepting and rejecting methodologies, techniques, practices. Much of all this is now redundant, and few would repeat my path. There was despair and hope, successes and moments of hopelessness, there were weeks and even months of vacuum, but I have never betrayed my faith in the direction towards the goal. Sport played a major role in my firm determination and consistency. From the perspective of time, I see that all this was so that YOU would be noticed, to initiate YOU into the secret, to test YOU. This is my understanding of the gift. THEY choose us, but we must make it so that they notice us, to impress THEM with faith, consistency, steadfastness, morality. I was given a LIGHTGRAM DIA TERRA to be a conduit between the Light Powers and my followers. Purified from religion, it is based on time-established theories and philosophical understandings about the essence of the laws of the Universe, about their universality. It does not conflict with established spiritual systems. Everyone must feel its effect for themselves, depending on their character, sensitivity, strength, consistency, purity of consciousness, responsibility. Lightgram Dia Terra is able to answer all spiritual quests, enriching them with an extremely precise practice.

R. Aleksandrova: - How does your working day go? Rhythm, ebbs and flows...
Dr. Dincho Chobanov: - My everyday life is full of touching to human destinies. Many people seek my help, I extend a hand to anyone who seeks my support. I have accepted the idea that pain originates on an energy and spiritual level, and then is projected onto the physical body level. In the construction of my system, I have set 14 levels of our health problems on a physical level and 14 on an energy level. These are deep levels in the cell that are activated at different stages of the diseases. I have set up my entire quantum treatment system according to them. This is how I work with people - in search, finding or directing to research through traditional medicine.
R Aleksandrova: - Do you spread the knowledge that is given to you from "above"?
Dr. Dincho Chobanov: - This unconventional method of mine for dealing with health problems are interesting for many people who have embarked on a similar path. I have quite a few groups throughout the country, I train them through seminars, periodic practices, dissemination of my theoretical and practical developments and techniques for maintaining the three areas of health:
- the physical - through forms of motor activity, body positions, rhythm, body conditioning;
- the energetic - through meditation, breathing, creating mandalas, sharing mathematical algorithms, mantras;
- the spiritual - through sacred texts, creative impulses - expressing the "inner" Self through external expression - drawing, poems, wisdom.
R Aleksandrova: - What do you think is the most important: gratitude, forgiveness or acceptance! And where is Love?
Dr. Dincho Chobanov: - Everything is important. Gratitude connects us with Divine gratitude, Forgiveness - with the state of our eternal Spirit, Love - directly with God. It is no coincidence that we have 3 hearts and 9 brains - this is only found in octopuses. Each of these 12 entities participates in the above categories in its own vibrational way - to love and be loved, to create, to be one with Creation, to actively participate in all processes in the Universe, in all its dimensions, spaces, times and lives. This makes us unique. Of course, if we successfully use this gift of ours.

R Aleksandrova: - What about morality? What do you think is moral in the context of your talent?

Dr. Dincho Chobanov: - Morality is leading. A person with a gift is also a person. The possibilities and impossibility of accomplishing something are a certain human condition. Which the healer must first admit internally, and then externally.

I believe that our three-layer health is the fruit of our inner understanding of our significance in the Universe, of our participation in building the universal models. Accepting these laws for myself, I try to radiate them and thus philosophically accept both our good and troubling states.

It very often happens that I direct the patient to the traditional together with the non-traditional treatment to achieve balance and harmony in the treated.

R Aleksandrova: - If you agree that our time is very special, what for you is the most special?

Dr. Dincho Chobanov: - In my opinion, a time has come that divides people: a time of purely material wanderings, of purely energetic ones and their symbiosis. The time has come to use matter only as an object for the study of spirit and energy. A time in which we must find the balance between the three categories and thus come to know our Divine beginning and essence.

R. Aleksandrova: - Would you like to share something personal about your unique method?

Dr. Dincho Chobanov: - I never seek gratitude, repayment, reward, dependence. This was suggested to me by the Energy with which I am in harmony, my Spiritual Guide. I have many examples that prove that this is the Path of the true healer.

R. Aleksandrova: - What advice can you give to our readers if they decide to self-heal and improve spiritually? And the connection between the two?

Dr. Dincho Chobanov: - They should be truly motivated, with a lot of knowledge, with the right methodology, with a trusted assistant and with Divine faith!

R Aleksandrova: - I can't help asking you the question, what is the place of Poetry in your life?

Dr. Dincho Chobanov: - When a person is in the "FIELD", then he is aware as part of the Divine consciousness. In my opinion, the Primary Wave of Creation is the bearer of all our answers, possibilities, gifts. The ordered rhythmic thought is the music of Creation, and Poetry - one of its means of expression. I was surprised when I started writing poems, but at a later stage my explanation for this talent of mine came. That's how I published my poetry collection PRINCIPLES AND RHYTHMS, which is part of my methodology for energy healing.

DEAR DR. DINCHO CHOBANOV, WORDS THANK YOU!

The interview was conducted by: Rozalia Aleksandrova

Author of collage: Ljiljana Stjelja, Serbia

Prodigy Magazine - March 2025

HOPE
SELF-HEALING

Prodigy Magazine - March 2025

As a preface to our new column SELF-HEALING, I'm more than happy to stimulate your curiosity for this topic, by giving away a free workbook of my
INTRODUCTION TO 4 STEPS TEACHING OF SELF-HEALING!
You'll be shocked, how easy, but powerful this method is!
Become your own self-healer in just one week!
Almost forgotten, ancient Chinese methods of self-healing are redesigned for launching as a huge contribution to humanity...
This should be a roadmap on your pathway to reach a natural ability of development in terms of using your own phisycal, mental resources, dealing with energetic field, reaching a sinchronicity and balance between body, mind, and spirit.
Click here for free ebook:

https://www.prodigylife.net/products/e-book-introduction-to-4-steps-teaching-of-self-healing?utm_source=copyToPasteBoard&utm_medium=product-links&utm_content=web

https://prodigy-life-program.myshopify.com/cart/5851765211174:1?channel=buy_button

Hopefully, it will help you to go deeper, and help you to become your own SELF-HEALER!
4 STEPS TEACHING OF SELF-HEALING
Ancient Chinese methods of self-healing enhanced bye mental exercises
https://prodigy-life-program.myshopify.com/cart/5863086129190:1?channel=buy_button

PRODIGY LIFE: Revolutionary way of self-development:

https://prodigy-life-program.myshopify.com/cart/5863111131174:1?channel=buy_button

©® **Zlatan Demirović**

Dr. ANA STJELJA, (ANA S. GAD), Serbia

FAEZE MOHAMMED HASSAN: Art as a Path to Healing

Faeze Mohammed Hassan's art is deeply rooted in Emirati heritage while embracing contemporary influences. She began her journey as a self-taught artist, transitioning from impressionism to realism, where she developed a distinctive style characterized by rich ochre tones and intricate details that evoke warmth and tradition. Her work often explores themes of cultural identity, history, and the evolving landscape of the UAE, merging past and present in a visually striking way. Inspired by orientalist painters like Gustav Bauernfeind, she integrates detailed architectural elements and figures into her compositions, creating narratives that resonate both locally and internationally. One of her most acclaimed pieces, *Monica Belucci*, won recognition at the 2024 Peru Bienal, showcasing her mastery of portraiture and her ability to capture contrast and elegance. She is also known for her dynamic cityscapes, such as her interpretation of the Dubai skyline, where she blends realism with an almost dreamlike quality, highlighting the balance between heritage and modernity. Her exhibitions, including a solo show at the Four Seasons Abu Dhabi, celebrate the role of Emirati women and their contributions to society. Lately, she has been exploring the intersection of art and technology, incorporating AI into her creative process to push the boundaries of traditional artistic expression. Actively involved in the cultural scene, she has participated in prestigious events such as **ADIHEX 2024**, the **National Day celebration at the Kuwait Embassy**, and numerous exhibitions across **Dubai, Abu Dhabi, Sharjah, and internationally**. Her work has also gained global recognition, having been featured in several international magazines, further establishing her as a significant voice in the contemporary art world. Her participation in the **UNESCO workshop in Sharjah** highlights her commitment to cultural preservation and artistic innovation, as she continues to engage in dialogues that bridge art, technology, and heritage. Looking ahead, she is set to participate in **World Art Dubai 2025**, the most prestigious art event in the UAE and the region, further solidifying her presence among leading contemporary artists. Through her dedication to both her craft and cultural storytelling, Faeze continues to shape the UAE's artistic landscape.

Mysticism and Magic Revealed in the novel "The Red Island" by Dr. Adil Alzarooni

In Dr. Adil Alzarooni's debut novel The Red Island: The Gatekeeper, the mystical and magical elements come alive as the protagonist journeys through a world where reality and the supernatural intertwine. Set in the abandoned Al Jazirah Al Hamra, the story delves into the life of an Emirati man navigating the cultural shifts while uncovering ancient secrets and facing mystical forces that shape his "The Red Island" tells stories of love, family, and friendships; of trauma, betrayal and loss; and of identity and fear of the other, as shaped by culture and politics. The novel has been written with the desire to build a brand new fantasy world, doused in Arabic and Islamic culture The novel beautifully blends fantasy, romance, and cultural identity, inviting readers into a realm where hidden gateways and powerful forces reveal truths about love, loss, and self-discovery. As the protagonist wrestles with personal and supernatural challenges, the novel offers a captivating exploration of a world where magic pulses beneath the surface of everyday life, making The Red Island a spellbinding tale that transcends time and place.

The real "Red Island" in the UAE is a reference to Al Jazirah Al Hamra, a historically significant and abandoned village located in the Emirate of Ras Al Khaimah. This area, known for its eerie and haunting atmosphere, is often referred to as the "Red Island" due to its striking red-hued sands and the color of the coral stone buildings that were once a part of the village. Al Jazirah Al Hamra was once a thriving community, with its inhabitants primarily involved in fishing, pearl diving, and trading. However, in the 1960s, the village was abandoned, and the area has remained deserted ever since. Today, it stands as a ghost town, offering visitors a glimpse into the UAE's past. The island is known for its preserved architecture, including traditional homes, mosques, and a coral stone fort. The mysterious ambiance and historical significance of Al Jazirah Al Hamra make it a popular site for tourists and photographers, often evoking a sense of the supernatural, making it a fitting inspiration for stories steeped in mysticism and magic.

©® **Ana Stjelja, (Ana S. Gad)**

FOLAJIMI NOTCH SHOAGA, Nigeria

SELF-HEALING ON HOPE

The reality of its literature is as its life science as ever since of the beginning, which is an evolution of its own process, getting it right is through determination that is truly focused on as it is its nature amidst natural human endowments having faith and deeds of great value worth living for personally and in extension to humanities as a sane sense of responsible creature.
Instances can be drawn from life hurdles, yet application of human experience differs in content and contextual true literature that has no stream of fallacy. Having hope towards life survival inter alia existence had gone through thorough process which even goes through different planning stage; like if a particular plan been hoped for did not work out, definitely the chances of other plans will be rely on for life survival while the pursuance of first plan continues its solution process.

With my stand as an authority of note through test of time, and time after time i had went through this process without any forms of fallacy or destructions. Like someone that has colour blindness, for me i can see the rainbow vividly which i had viewed its true literature severally as a natural sign of hope and indestructible lives of humans and its evolution. Even at distant in view of another nature, an iridescent existence can be observed as an established fact of life through an animal like birds having such light in its feathers.

Note that universally hope is a very strong bond of human minds and to be candid not for someone being desultory in nature, and for those that believes its comprehensiveness it really has to do with faith and deeds of one's personal life and expectations in terms of needs at whichever level of brow human finds or discovered himself or herself.

©® **Folajimi Notch Shoaga**

FROSINA TASEVSKA, Macedonia

PERSISTENCE IN THE FIELD OF THOUGHT

Just as all living things in nature thrive on rhythm, our bodies also need a harmonious flow to prepare for upcoming challenges and opportunities effectively. Embracing this natural rhythm allows for smoother transitions between different phases of our lives. To cultivate authentic inner stability, calmness, and strength, it is essential for our lives to develop an optimal rhythm. This rhythm plays a vital role in unlocking our most profound qualities. For many, the absence of a consistent life rhythm poses a significant challenge, leading to ongoing difficulties in managing thoughts, emotions, ideas, and creative abilities. By committing ourselves to persistent effort and action, we can establish a rhythm that paves the way to our highest virtues and capacities. Embracing this commitment empowers us to elevate our existence and fully realize our potential. Our thoughts serve as a powerful and boundless reservoir that shapes our perception of both visible and invisible realities. They have a profound impact on our relationships and our comprehension of the deeper laws and meanings of existence. In an ideal world, our thinking would offer an accurate and objective perspective of the world; however, reality often diverges from this ideal. More often than not, our thoughts can mislead us, creating illusions and distorting our understanding of events and experiences. Thus, embracing clarity in our thinking is essential for achieving genuine understanding and nurturing meaningful connections in life. Hence, our perseverance should be focused on learning to avoid the most common and perilous traps that we often encounter. These traps can be seen as "circles." Whenever we find ourselves ensnared in a "circle" that leads to repetitive conclusions and reactions, it becomes crucial to develop the persistence and willpower necessary to break free from this detrimental cycle. Instead of endlessly ruminating on the same thoughts - which only perpetuate our current mindset and emotional state - we should consciously strive to pause and redirect our focus. To attain genuine understanding, we must go beyond mere willpower; a heartfelt desire is crucial to ensure that our conclusions resonate with truth and righteousness, rather than merely mirroring our own desires. Our persistence in thought must delve deeper. In this pursuit, profound, sincere love and genuine kindness become not just important, but essential. Ultimately, this dedication to higher values remains fundamental across all facets of life.

©® **Frosina Tasevska**

S AFROSE, Bangladesh

BE POSITIVE

Be positive. Think positive. Take positively. If there's nothing to be in your favor, just take as a part of the exam board.
You're the part of this exam. Never mind. Just go and catch your sight on the board. Remember, after night day will come. Dark night can't cover your life all time. It will be over very soon. Then you can see the ray of sun. That's the beginning stage of the new day. So, don't scared. You must beat your fear.
Life is only one. This earth is here. You are here. Also, your dream, destination. Apart these, so many collisions, hindrances. Everything is possible or not, depending on your possession. How can you accept?
Be careful. Life is beautiful. Don't be silly to take any unwanted decision. You can't reach your dream. You can't wipe your tears. Who tells? Rubbish talks.
Listen, find out yourself. Your inner spirit.
You have a magical mind. You can do anything if you want. Try to smile. Can't? Then, you may be the dumb one. You fail to feel the beats of heart. Don't you know? Your beautiful heart. It loves all. It Scatters ray of sweet love. Love can defend anything. So?
Chill dear. Life is a swing. Ups-downs continue. You just enjoy the reel.
Without pain, can't be achieved the soothing gem of happiness.
Be yourself with love. Be positive for each step. Fallen tears must be for the winning smile.

©® **S Afrose**

FARZANEH DORRI, Iran/Denmark

THOUGHTS AND FEELINGS

Thoughts are one thing and feelings are another. But when they are experienced at the same time over and over again, the brain can fuse them together so that the thought is experienced as a feeling. This means that every time we think a thought, an emotion follows. This does not have to be a problem, but it can also create triggers.

We constantly mix thoughts and feelings together, without noticing it. Unfortunately, this can also lead to some negative thoughts about ourselves involuntarily bringing negative emotions with them. Then it feels as if the thought itself hurts.

In addition to us linguistically mixing things up, thoughts can affect us emotionally. We can get an unpleasant feeling if we think about something unpleasant. For example, if we hear about an accident. Or

we are emotionally affected by hearing about another tragedy. Here we use both our ability to empathize with how others feel and our ability to have compassion. This is good and it defines us as human beings.

We can also think about something without feeling anything at the same time. If you think about the mathematical formula of Pythagoras, it can be accompanied by a completely neutral feeling, because it is

just mathematics. Or it can be accompanied by a feeling of panic, if you try unsuccessfully to think of it for an oral exam. Feelings depend entirely on the context, but thoughts are free.

Thoughts are thoughts. They are thoughts about the world. We can think in images, we can think in sound and we think especially in words, because we are so linguistic. Sometimes it is very clear that this is what is happening. We can create the feeling of what we are thinking about. We can create the feeling of lying in the sunshine in

Mallorca, we can create the feeling of having a good dinner at the restaurant. This means that we can look forward to it in advance.

So we can create feelings from our thoughts. This is both good and bad. We can be happy when we think about the children's wedding, or scared when we think about the driving test.

Often it happens so quickly that it is impossible to know which came first. The thought or the feeling. And it is often experienced as if the thought is the feeling. But the more you look, the clearer it is that it is different.

When you practice mindfulness, you strengthen, among other things, your ability to sense. Through meditation, you train to be able to distinguish more details in your senses and to be able to separate senses and separate senses, feelings and thoughts. By training to observe and separate your senses, feelings and thoughts neutrally, you become able to experience thoughts and sensory impressions separately from feelings.

We tend to react instinctively to our trigger thoughts because we experience them as if they are also a feeling. And then we do something about those thoughts - we suppress or avoid the thoughts. But brain science tells us that this makes the thoughts more frequent. And then a context arises - it is experienced as if we cannot control the thoughts. And this can lead to more negative feelings. Which in turn are mixed with thoughts. The thoughts run in circles and they activate negative feelings.

The solution, just like in mindfulness, is to separate thoughts from emotions. You don't have to meditate to do this. However, metacognitive therapy uses some exercises inspired by mindfulness. Detached attention can be trained. And the very act of being able to control your attention, to change focus, can also be trained with simple exercises.

Both help to separate thoughts and emotions and make you feel better about your thoughts. This is what is meant by the fact that in metacognitive therapy you don't change the content of your thoughts - but you change your relationship to your thoughts.

At the same time as training in separation and detachment, it is also important to become more aware of your thought patterns and thought strategies. You discover the connections between how you use your thoughts - which thoughts you pursue - which thoughts you feel. This is also an important part of what happens in metacognitive therapy.

Ultimately, it is about separating thoughts from emotions and getting your choice back.

©® **Farzaneh Dorri**

Made in the USA
Las Vegas, NV
16 March 2025